T0209462

Also by the author:

TWICE UPON A TIME, Moody Press
IN GOD'S HAND, Chalice Press
A FRESH WIND IN YOUR SAILS, West Bow Press

To Love in Return

Donald D. McCall

WESTBOW
PRESS®
A DIVISION OF THOMAS NELSON
& ZONDERVAN

This book is a work of non-fiction. Unless otherwise noted, the author and the publisher make no explicit guarantees as to the accuracy of the information contained in this book and in some cases, names of people and places have been altered to protect their privacy.

WestBow Press books may be ordered through booksellers or by contacting:

WestBow Press
A Division of Thomas Nelson & Zondervan
1663 Liberty Drive
Bloomington, IN 47403
www.westbowpress.com
1 (866) 928-1240

Because of the dynamic nature of the Internet, any web addresses or links contained in this book may have changed since publication and may no longer be valid. The views expressed in this work are solely those of the author and do not necessarily reflect the views of the publisher, and the publisher hereby disclaims any responsibility for them.

Any people depicted in stock imagery provided by Getty Images are models, and such images are being used for illustrative purposes only. Certain stock imagery © Getty Images.

Scripture quotations are] from the New Revised Standard Version Bible, copyright © 1989 the Division of Christian Education of the National Council of the Churches of Christ in the United States of America. Used by permission. All rights reserved.

Scripture taken from the King James Version of the Bible.

ISBN: 978-1-9736-7151-0 (sc)
ISBN: 978-1-9736-7152-7 (hc)
ISBN: 978-1-9736-7150-3 (e)

Library of Congress Control Number: 2019911239

Print information available on the last page.

WestBow Press rev. date: 08/15/2019

Dedicated to my daughter
Katherine McCall Isles

Previously published and quoted articles
From The Presbyterian Outlook:
PNC Poem
Minister Appreciation Month
How Prison Changed My Preaching

All scriptures taken from NRSV unless otherwise cited.
All poems written by Donald D. McCall

Contents

(Many of these chapters originated as letters to my children.)

$\mathcal{P}$reface

This is my daughter Katherine. This is also how I will always remember her. Bone of my bone. Flesh of my flesh. Heart of my own heart. When she would lie on my chest at the end of a long day of playing I would let her just lie there until I could sense that her heavy breathing had calmed down and then I would lift her up and carry her to the foot of the stairs leading up to her second floor bedroom. At that point I would shift her weight so that she would automatically put her arms around my neck and then I would slowly climb the stairs, telling her at each step how much I loved her and slowly giving her a few love pats on her back. It was a ritual that I loved and I sensed that in some mystical way she was aware of what I was saying and doing. What child doesn't love being hugged to bed. As we climbed the stairs I could occasionally sense her squeeze her arms around my neck…not for safety reasons but rather as a response to the feelings of loving security she was experiencing. However I always felt that they were more than reflective responses.

One night as I was carrying her up the stairs and patting her three times on her back to emphasize the universal language of "I Love You" I suddenly felt her release her right hand's grip from around my neck and then I sensed the gentlest tapping of her small hand three times on my back. I suddenly realized that *it was love responding to Love in return.* It was one of the most exciting moments in my life. I was over whelmed with emotion and sat down on that same step and just held her in my arms. I realized for the first time in my life that she knew how much I loved her and she was responding to that love with her love in return.

Scripture teaches us that to Love is one of the penultimate of life's experiences. And so it is. But Jesus also teaches us that 'Being Loved in Return' provides the ultimate height of human love. After His resurrection Jesus met his disciples at daybreak on the shore of the Sea of Galilee and He made a small fire for them to share His breakfast with them. (John 21) After they had eaten, He turned to Peter and asked him the most quintessential question of life: "Peter, do you love me?" It was life's final and ultimate question. The whole of the Bible is history of God expressing his Love for us. The whole of the New Testament is God expressing His love for us in and through the life of Jesus Christ. It therefore becomes consequentially that the whole meaning of our lives lies is in our answering that question. Have we yet learned **to Love in Return?**

When you do first sense that Love in Return it is a breathtaking experience. You will have to sit down as I did on the steps and regain your balance and reconstruct your understanding of the impact of Loving and being Loved in Return. And that is what this book is all about!

Donald D. McCall

To Love and Be Loved in Return
John 21:15

I was 17 tears old. A freshman at Lafayette College over 1200 miles from home. My father graduated from Lafayette as did my brother but I was ambivalent about spending the next four years of my life at an all-male college with students who weren't any brighter than I was, but who were infinitely wealthier than I was and who could afford to have cars and date girls from Bryn Mawr and Vassar. In the springtime of that year I was walking across the quad from the Student Union to my dorm and I started humming the last song I heard at the Student Union. It was "Nature Boy" by Nat King Cole. I can still hear it's haunting refrain. It is a song of a wise young boy who,

> "… Spoke of many things
> Fools and Kings
> This he said to me
> The greatest thing you'll ever learn
> Is just to love and be loved in return"

That song stayed with me until the end of the semester at which time I left college to wander very far over land and sea to learn how to "**Love and be Loved**". I caught a bus to New York City and went down to the docks at west 42nd street to sign on as crew for the next freighter that was sailing anywhere. Not having 'Merchant Seaman' papers I was advised to go to Philadelphia to try to sign on a stateside gulf coast 'Oil Tanker'. That too failed to work out and ultimately I joined the US Navy and found myself on a Navy Destroyer in the Pacific. I loved it and was well cared for (not loved, but well cared for) in return.

After the Korean War I returned home and decided to go to college where my father was on the faculty. I enjoyed his presence in my life, in the classroom, on the golf course and in our daily discussions. I admired him greatly and he served as a role model for me throughout my life. I also knew that deep down he loved me too. But it wasn't the kind of love that Nat King Cole was singing about when I was a Freshman at Lafayette.

I also went to chapel every Wednesday on campus and to church every Sunday Morning. More to check out the girls in the choir than the text in the sermon. I knew since childhood that Jesus loved me. But I also knew that Jesus loved 'everyone' and therefore I never felt that his contact with me was anything more than an institutional relationship. Nothing personal. Even as I child I used to ask my mother, (as do all children) "Do you Love me?" She would always answer, "Oh, you know that Dad and I love you boys....there isn't a thing **we** wouldn't do for you." Not exactly the question I was asking … nor the answer I was looking for. I wasn't seeking to be part of a **package deal** …either at home or with Jesus at the church.

When I went to Princeton I eagerly looked forward to establishing a deeper and more personal relationship with the Jesus that I had read about but never knew. I read voraciously. Studied vigorously, prayed earnestly. But I gradually grew bored with Latin, Hebrew, Greek, Barth, Brunner and Calvin. Then I discovered Bonhoeffer, Kierkegaard and Tillich. Especially Tillich whose theme was: *"God accepts you; all you have to do is accept being accepted"* Yes, I thought, the New Testament is not so much about telling us that God Loves us as, it is a question asking us if we love God in return.

It is possible not to accept God's love. It's possible to be loved by

Donald D. McCall

someone and not to accept that love and share it in return. Nat King Cole was right…It's possible to love and **not** to be loved in return … and therein all life loses its meaning. At that point I began reading the Gospels differently. It wasn't all so much about God's loving me but **more about my Loving Him in return.**

At the end of His life, as recorded in John's Gospel, Jesus asks Peter one question…a final question….life's ultimate question. He took Peter aside and asked him, "Simon, Son of John, Do you love me?' (John 21:15) Three times He asked him the same question. It is the quintessential and final question of the Gospel. For years I have read it from pulpit and podium with the emphasis on the word LOVE. "Do you **LOVE** me? Thinking that Love was the heart and core of the Gospel.

And now, toward the end of my life I have come to realize and to understand that the emphasis should not be on the word LOVE but rather on the word ME. Read it (out Loud, and to yourself) with the emphasis on the last word: "Simon, son of John, Do you love ME?". It's not a question about 'Loving'. It's a question about being loved in return! It's about entering into a personal relationship with Jesus of Nazareth… an encounter in which you respond to LOVE with love in return. I'm glad that I've lived long enough to learn, to understand, to experience and especially to respond to Love with **Love in RETURN** ….

*T*he Left Hand Of God

I was standing (actually, I was leaning heavily on my cane) at the narthex door anticipating that hazardous walk down the sloping floor to my pew when **Jim Spilburg** (everybody's best friend at church) walked up behind me and putting his right hand on my left shoulder quietly asked, "Do you need some help?" It wasn't what he said that took me by surprise…it was the touch of his hand upon my shoulder. I'd felt that hand on my shoulder before. It was when I was 17 years of age serving on board a Navy Destroyer during the Korean War. We had tied up at a Naval Base for minor repairs and I attended the base chapel the first Sunday I was there. It had been sometime since I had been to a church. Upon leaving the chapel that morning everyone received a small wallet sized picture as a remembrance of Christ's presence in our lives. As you can see, I still have mine! It wasn't what **Jim** said to me that Sunday morning that startled me It was his hand on my left shoulder. It felt to me as though it was the same hand that had vouchsafed me throughout those tumultuous years of my Navy life and which was now resting upon me as I stood (leaning on my cane) at the Narthex door.

Years before, when I was a grad student at Princeton, as I was **walking one night** across campus to the Firestone library I began wondering to myself if I was there at Seminary because I wanted to be there and loved being there so much … or if I was

Donald D. McCall

in some way 'Called' to ministry. Every Divinity student faces this dilemma ...repeatedly. In the quiet of that evening as I walked alone I began to sense that I wasn't alone. I felt the pressure of a strong hand upon my left shoulder. I didn't turn around to look. Not a word was spoken. But I knew that His hand was upon my shoulder urging me on. It was more than just a feeling ... it was a conviction.

As the years went on I began to realize how often Jesus changed peoples lives by **simply reaching out to touch** them with his hands. Sometimes, more than His words, His hands were the source of his helping, guiding or healing. How often we read of his reaching out and touching those in need. A <u>leper</u> in Galilee; <u>Peter's mother in law</u> in Capernaum; <u>Two blind men</u> that were led to Him; a <u>deaf man</u> in Decapolis; Another <u>blind man</u> in Bethsaida; and <u>another</u> in Jerusalem; a <u>woman</u> with osteoporosis; a <u>soldier</u> whose ear had been cut off in the Garden of Gethsemane; and on and on. In my many years of ministry, I have come to believe that Jesus still touches our lives in many of our daily interactions. That's why we 'lay hands' on those ordained to religious orders. I well remember my ordination and I knew who it was in that crowd behind me that was pressing his hand down on my left shoulder. It was Dr. Kessler, the Moderator of the General Assembly and he didn't want me to ever forget the moment!

This is <u>not</u> an account that I share with everybody, but in approaching my own death I want these truths to pass from my life on to you. Recently I have felt more and more the hands of Christ reaching out to me. A few Sundays ago as I was listening intently to the organ postlude, a woman about my age who was sitting across the aisle and behind me, rose up and walked slowly over to me and gently **placed her hand** on my left shoulder and said, "You're looking so sad...are you alright?" I responded " I was just thinking about my Father. He used to chide me (and keep me humble) by saying that he loved the Postlude as the best part of the worship service... I miss him." Then I thanked her for reaching out and sharing my sadness.

One Communion Sunday as I struggled to rise up out of my pew to walk forward down the aisle I felt Betsy who was walking behind me surreptitiously take hold of my belt loop with her **hand** to guide me on my wobbly way. Then half way towards the chancel Dick Lovell walking alongside me reached over and unobtrusively took my **left hand** and kept me steadily on course as we approached the communion elements. I realized that morning that I had received more than the gift of the bread and the cup. When we returned to our places in our pew granddaughter Claire was sitting next to me. When the minister began the Prayer of Thanksgiving Claire reached over, took my hand, and held it throughout the prayer. To me it was a moment as beautiful as any moment that Jesus ever reached out his hand to touch, heal, help or pray with those whose life stories are recorded in Scripture.

Just a month ago as I was walking up the center aisle to exit after the service I noticed that Barb was lagging behind speaking to Joanne Schalch. Noticing their **hand** gestures I presumed it was another knitting conversation. I went on ahead but when I looked back I noticed that they were embracing. I mentioned it to Barb on the way home and Barb responded that Joanne had stopped talking and just stood there and embraced her for the longest time without saying a word. Joanne died a week later. I am sure that God's hand was upon them both and embracing them with His Love even as *it embraces you now.*

Donald D. McCall

Fig Trees Were Not Made For Shade

A man had a fig tree planted in his vineyard: he came looking for fruit on it and found none. So he said to the gardener, "See here, For three years I have come looking for fruit on this fig tree, and still I have none. Cut it down, why should it be wasting the soil? Luke 13:6-7

They were studying the Gospel of Luke…in depth. The teacher asked a class member to read aloud the parable of the barren fig tree in Chapter 13 so that every class member would hear it in the words of the same translation. It was the story of the owner of a fig tree who had been looking for fruit from the tree for some time and the tree still wasn't productive. So he told the gardener to cut it down because it was no longer productive and thus it was wasting the soil in which it was planted.

Then the teacher asked the class members what they thought of the parable that Jesus had shared with them. They responded quickly and enthusiastically. Some said that it meant that God had given us a purpose in life and that we needed to be true to our calling. Others said that it spoke to them of the need to be more industrious and productive than we are. Some said that it meant that we should live for others by generating in our lives a product for the sustenance of others. Fruit for others to eat.

Then an older member of the class spoke up. He had long been retired from the ministry and his years of productivity were almost beyond his memory. He said, "I find this parable terribly threatening. I realize that I am no longer productive and I have no hope of ever being productive again. Therefore I sense that this parable is telling me that I am no longer worth taking up the place ...the soil upon which I exist. And that I need to be cut down. That my life needs to be ended....and that's frightening!"

"OH NO!" cried out all the class members. You're very important to us. To be sure, your lifetime career may have ended, but we enjoy you here. You're productive in a different way. You always put a different **shade** of light on what we are studying."

Now upon hearing that response, Jesus, who unbeknownst to the class had been standing out in the hallway listening to the class discussions, looked up to heaven and said half out loud: "Different **shade? Shade?** I was talking about a fig tree....Fig trees were created to produce figs, not shade!" And then shaking his head he muttered something to the effect that he couldn't believe how his simple story of a barren fig tree could be so overly complicated and so difficult for modern hearers to understand. Then he walked down the hall to see how the ladies at the church rummage sale were getting along,

As he turned the corner in the hallway, he looked up to heaven one last time and with tongue in cheek (which was hard for him to do) he said, "Even my simplest parables seem to be too profound. But frankly, I can't wait till next week to hear the class explain how that lost coin was found !"

Donald D. McCall

Spontaneity

When I was the Pastor of the First Presbyterian Church in Rochester I received a phone call one morning from the Embassy of Liberia in Washington D.C. It was in the 1980's after a coup d'etat in Liberia had taken place and the Embassy was calling to tell me that the Prime Minister of Liberia was scheduled for a serious surgical appointment at the Mayo Clinic and being fearful of another assassination attempt would it be possible for me to arrange private housing and transportation for the PM's delegation among the members of my congregation to avoid the publicity of their staying in a local hotel.

My response was **instinctive** and **spontaneous.** The Presbyterian Church has had a strong and positive relationship with Liberia since its first Missionary endeavors in 1847 Much of the modern leadership in Liberia has risen out of Presbyterian Mission Schools. I felt like it was having our extended family coming to town for a visit. I announced the need to the congregation and by week's end we had homes assigned for every member of the delegation (about 14 including bodyguards) and Bank President John Cochran had made arrangements for their financial money changing transactions. It wasn't long before 'distant cousins' became a part of our family.... although some previously scheduled events in our lives had to be changed. One event that I will never forget was that I had forgotten that Dr. and Mrs. Fleming had invited me for a dinner gathering at their home. I called Teresa and told her that the PM of Liberia was my guest and asked if I could bring him along (and his two bodyguards). She graciously allowed that it would be a pleasure to add them to her already long list of guests.

I called her again the next day and with embarrassment asked her if my daughter who was driving down from Minneapolis for the weekend could also join us. Teresa laughed and said "Of course. She was always our favourite baby sitter! We'll make room." Indeed they did! When we arrived that night I could see that Teresa had opened the French doors between the dining room and the living room and stretched out the dinner table into half the width of their stately home. What a wonderful evening it was! While we were eating desert I overheard Teresa say to the PM, "I noticed that you were staring at my table decorations. (she had wrought iron apple tree stands at both ends of the extended table laden with fresh apples.) She asked, "Do you like them?" The Prime Minister answered, "Oh yes…very much. Then very slowly he said: "You know, in our country we eat them."

After his return to Liberia the PM sent me a beautiful 'Thank You' letter of which the following is but a part:

> "For all of your humanitarian assistances I thank you and the whole congregation of the church…At home there are many people who wish to propitiate my official grace and consideration. For the people of your church there was nothing they wanted except **to help someone in need**. Your kindness to me was therefore pure and **spontaneous**. I, therefore invoke the blessings of God upon all of you."

Through that brief encounter with the PM of Liberia and his delegation I learned one of life's most important lessons. I came to understand that '**Spontaniety**' was one of the most important aspects

Donald D. McCall

of discipleship. Acts of charity and Love are not generated through committee actions as much as they are the result of instinctive and spontaneous responses of one heart to another. I say this because our church in Madison has just gone through an eight month period of discernment to decide whether or not we want to be 'Sanctuary Congregation".

We have a young Associate Pastor whom I admire greatly for his personal commitment to his 'High Calling" who has spearheaded this magnanimous quest **to help a societal group in need.** In a straw vote the congregation followed his lead and voted 66% in favor of becoming a "Sanctuary Congregation". However the Session later voted against it. My concern isn't the decision of the Session but rather a personal concern that the Session's negative vote might have squelched a young pastor's spontaneous enthusiasm and zeal. Lengthy months of deliberation can do that. I fear that in our desire to do all things "Decently and in Order" we all too often squash the spirit of spontaneity that lies ready to spring forth in our dreams. In my heart I have come to believe that '**Spontaniety**' is at the very heart of discipleship. It pops up on every page of Scripture. I cite the following cases:

When Jesus first called his disciples they spontaneously drop their fishing nets and followed Him. No 8 month deliberation there! When Jesus calls Peter to step out if the boat on the Sea of Galilee, Peter spontaneously responds (and begins to sink). No testing of the waters first! When a woman spontaneously anointed Jesus with rare perfume there was no premeditated counting of the cost! In the Garden of Gethsemane when in the course of His betrayal and arrest a soldier's ear was cut off, Jesus instantly, lovingly, and spontaneously restored the soldiers ear. Spontaneity is at the heart of Christ's love for us.

I remember when Barb was elected to the Church Session here at Madison. The new elders gathered in front of the chancel at the service's end and were publicly installed. Then they marched out in single file behind the clergy for a public reception in the Narthex. As

Barb walked past the pew I was sitting in she **spontaneously** broke ranks and leaned in and gave me a big kiss on the forehead and then she jumped quickly back into ranks.

I thought to myself, *"It's that kind of a spontaneous relationship that Christ wants to have with us !"*

"Through sloth the roof sinks in...and through indolence the building leaks"

Ecclesiastes 9:18

SLOTH

Ah Sloth, I know thee well
Thou and indolence, thy linguistic twin ...
For as the Scriptures do so clearly foretell
Thou art the cause of my roof falling in !

Inertia is your instant inclination
Which prompted me toward further procrastination
And though I wish there were some other explanation
Thou hast become the source of my barn's dilapidation.

Well, I hope to fix the roof...someday soon
But getting started is what's so very hard
Maybe I'll put it off until tomorrow afternoon
After I get an estimate from the lumberyard....

Ah, Sloth, once again you've done me in
Once again I fear that you and Indolence are going to win!
Whispering in my ear that this may not be a good time to begin
While allowing my Sloth to become the cause of my barn's ruin !

The Face Of God
Genesis 33:10

When I was a young boy, we would leave the hot city of Tripoli to spend our summers in the mountain village of Aley where it was delightfully cool all summer long. Every morning we had time set aside for reading. And every day we had lunch out on the veranda of our home which had a magnificent view of the valley below and the city of Beirut in the distance and the Mediterranean Sea extending into the horizon.

I remember one summer when my Father assigned us the reading of Victor Hugo's _Les Miserables_ (in French.) It was well over 1200 pages long! I was a faster reader than my brother and the book was so fascinating that I often couldn't wait for him to catch up so that I could read on into the next day's assignment. I recall vividly how thought provoking my Father's questions were each day at lunch as we dallied over our food and discussed our assigned reading passages and came to grips with the religious and social implications of all the plots and sub-plots of that great novel. I realize now how deeply my life was challenged by Hugo's insights expressed in the life of Jean Valjean.

Perhaps that is why I encouraged all of you to read Hugo when you were growing up, even though our dinner conversations were much more extrinsic in nature. But then, you are all of the generation when the play "Les Miz" became popular. It claimed one of the longest runs ever on Broadway and was a fairly accurate adaptation of the long novel written by Hugo. In one of the last scenes in the play Val jean gathers his family around his bedside and says, "And remember this truth, **'To love another person is to see the face of God."** That truth experienced in Valjean's life is affirmation of the Biblical account of Jacob and Esau in the Book of Genesis. After a long separation Jacob was about to meet his brother Esau. Jacob feared the meeting. After all, years earlier he had stolen Esau's birthright through deception and now he was <u>certain</u> <u>that</u> Esau would take his revenge. But when they met Esau approached Jacob not with anger but with-forgiveness. And they embraced and Jacob said, "To see your face is like seeing the face of God."

I have long loved the Finale of the play, <u>Les Miz</u> which combines the words of the novel with the Genesis story of Jacob and Esau. In the play, Cossette, Fantine and Eponine are gathered around Valjeaan's bedside as he is dying. Valjean says:

"Now you are here again beside me. Now I can die in peace, for now my life is blessed."

Cossette quickly responds, "You will live, Papa. You're going to live. It's too soon to ever say goodbye"

Valjean speaks: "Yes, Cossette, forbid me now to die. I'll obey...l"ll try."

And then later as the end draws near Valjean says: "Forgive me all my trespassses and take me to your Glory. Take my love for love is everlasting. And remember the truth that once was spoken: **To love another person is to see the face of God."**

I write all of this to you because I want to share a privileged communication with you. Every morning when I wake up, I look to my left and see Barb's face resting on her pillow and I say to myself, **"To love you is to see the face of God."** That's not sacrilege its sacrament... as Hugo and Jacob and I will attest...and it fixes the course of my day and my life.

$\mathcal{B}$eing Multilingual
Matthew 27:46

Dr. Elaine Pagels of Princeton University wrote a best-selling book in 1979 entitled **The Gnostic Gospels.** I read it as soon as the printer's ink dried on the pages of it's first edition. I was captivated. Her acquired knowledge (PhD Harvard) combined with her shared personal intuitions and experiences (the death of her young son and her husband within two years) made it fascinating to read. Her inclusion on the team that translated the Nag Hamadi Scrolls discovered in 1945 along the banks of the Nile River made it possible for her to write **The Gnostic Gospels** in which she presents new understanding of the great questions of our human existence in a theological language different from our own. In all, Dr. Pagels has written **8** books, all of which are on my bookshelf, with one that she autographed and inscribed to me which holds a place of honor in my heart. When I read recently that she had a new book due out this summer, I called Princeton to congratulate her, only to learn that her book 's publication date had been advanced to later in the fall.

Barbara and I had the opportunity to have lunch with Dr. Pagels a number of years ago and I remember her telling us how she had grown up in the church but had lost interest in religion in her teen-age years. Then in college she took a course in the Greek language and began reading the Gospels in the Greek text which proved to be a new experience for her which changed much of her thinking. I realized at that moment that I too had a translation of the New Testament that was written in a different language, sitting on my desk that has changed much of my thinking over the years. It's scalled the "**New Testament From Aramaic**" published in 1940 (and also autographed by it's editor George M. Lamsa). It's the New Testament translated from the language that Jesus spoke, which is also my 'mother tongue', the Arabic of my childhood. My father was a Presbyterian Missionary in the Near East and my brother and I were raised speaking Arabic, French and English. So more and more in later life I began to turn to different translations of the Bible to gain new understanding of the New Testament.

After my years in graduate school I decided to travel to Ein Gedi on the cliffs of the Dead Sea to learn more of the discovery of the Dead Sea Scrolls. These scrolls, found in the eleven caves at Qumran, are ancient Biblical manuscripts one thousand years older than any others previously acquired. That trip opened my mind to the importance of studying texts that were unknown when I was in seminary. Consequently, when Elaine Pagels published her book about the Gnostic Gospels which were discovered at Nag Hamadi, I immediately wanted to know more. So I began planning a trip to the historic site on the River Nile to discover for myself what had been published about these ancient texts.

When my daughter Kate saw the maps and articles laid out on my desk, she not only became curious but also became involved in the study of these recent discoveries. And naturally wanted to know if she could join me on this trip. I, of course, was more than delighted to have a travelling companion and a new scholar be at my side. So we flew to Cairo and traveled down the Nile to Luxor on the river which was adjacent to the Nag Hamadi site. After we arrived there and were situated, we had a free afternoon to get acclimated to our new research site. As we were walking down by the river I noticed a number of small boats called feluccas with lateen sails pulled up on the shore. I asked the owner of one these small sailboats if I could rent it from him for the afternoon. We haggled back and forth in Arabic, much to Kate's surprise. We finally came to an agreement about the price and he gave us permission to use his boat for an afternoon sail. Then Kate and I got into the boat to enjoy an afternoon on the Nile River. It was a magnificent sail, just the two of us floating down the Nile River. I thought to myself that everything will be anticlimactic after this!

The enormity of the discovery of eleven complete books and one thousand pages of fragments that are still being studied to this day.

For example: The Apostle Paul wrote the church in Corinth: "If I speak in the tongues of men and of angels but do not have love, I am a noisy gong or clanging cymbal" (I Cor. 13:1). And then Paul goes on to describe that 'love' in Greek words: phileo=brotherly love; Eros-Sensual love; Agape-altruistic love; Storge-family love. My Aramaic New Testament adds these words to the text: "but if I do not have love in my heart, I am a noisy...". Love in my heart is an Aramaic term derived from the root word "Hab" in the Old Testament best described as "Beloved" or as I always use in my salutation to you in my letters; "Ma Habibis". It is a love beyond the 4 Greek words for Love used in the New Testament. Beyond the words of the Marriage Service: "To have and to hold from this day forward...." which are words of power and control. The Aramaic "Love in my heart" is a Love that seeks only to empower and enfold. The Aramaic text gives me a new understanding of the word LOVE. I can live with that.

For example: I have always been bothered by the words of Jesus when he said, "Whoever does not hate his father, mother, children … cannot be my disciple." (Luke 14:26) Well frankly there is no way that I would ever come to hate my Father, Mother or my Children.

Donald D. McCall

On the contrary, I would willingly lay down my life for them. (which is incidentally what I did when I joined the Navy and take an oath to be willing to lay down my life to defend my country and my loved ones). The Aramaic New Testament translates the verse this way, "He who does not put aside his father…". I can live with the tenderness of the Aramaic translation. As life changes we all have to "put aside" some family responsibilities as we accept new ones. I can live with that.

I share these thoughts with you….not to minimize the sacredness of Holy Scripture…but rather to maximize the possibilities of new insights brought about through variant translations of Scripture. And to remind you that even though I am a Doctor of Divinity I want you to know that I am still struggling through the existential problems of my own human destiny.

Lastly, I want to share with you my greatest discovery at Nag Hamadi. It was after we had returned home to Rochester that friends were asking Kate, who had seen the pyramids, the Sphinx and the wonders of the ancient world, what had impressed her most from her trip. It's a question to be expected whenever you return home from any journey. I was anxious to hear her response. She said with a smile on her face, "What impressed me the most was that my Father was conversant in Arabic." I smiled to myself as I realized that I had discovered more about our relationship as a father and daughter than I had discovered about the artifacts at Nag Hamadi. I loved that!

$\mathcal{A}$ Present Day Anointing
Psalm 23

Barbara often (more often than not) chides (berates) me for my specificity (explicit use) of language ... whether it be my shifting from Latin to Hebrew to Greek to Aramaic or to French or to German ... all in order to preserve the original meaning of an intended word or thought. Recently she was asked to do a program on the gospel of Luke at church and knowing that I had studied under Dr. Caird when I was a student at Oxford, she asked me to ride along with her on the **8** hour drive to Omaha where she had a legal case and we could discuss the contents of Dr. Caird's textbook on Luke on the way. Who could resist such a pleasurable invitation? A few days later as we left Madison and got on the interstate. I opened Dr. Caird's book and started reading and discussing its 25 page Introduction. **8** hours later when we arrived in Omaha we were still discussing the Introduction!

After Barb concluded her court case in Omaha we started back on the **8** hour journey home to Madison. We picked up the account in Luke and moved through the first chapter until we came to the account of the **Baptism** of Jesus. At that point I veered off track from the baptism to the annointing of Jesus by the Holy Spirit at the Jordan. The annointing stemmed from a practice of the Shepherds in the land who were concerned that lice and other insects would get into the wool of the sheep. When the insects got near the sheep's head they could burrow into the sheep's ears and those slippery mites would enter into the sheep's ear canals. So the shepherds in ancient days poured oil over the sheep's head to stop the insect infestations which often killed the sheep by driving the poor little lambs mad. The sheep would bang their heads against the rocks to get the worms out, thereby sometimes killing themselves in the effort. So, the shepherds would annoint the sheep with oil which created a barrier of protection which kept those hideous little insects from burrowing into the sheep's ears. This concept of annointing the sheep eventually took on political and religious significance and became a symbol of consecration to special offices where royalty were annointed as well as Old Testament prophets and priests. The use of modern "sheep dip" is the equavilent of that long-ago shepherd's simple treatment of creating a barrier which protected the sheep from harming themselves. The annointing routine grew in significance and became a part of the baptismal rite where infants were annointed as part of the baptismal ritual, granting the recipient the power of a blessing as well as physical protection. The variations of that history of baptism and annointing have continued on down to this day.

My grandson **Xavier's** recent Baptism was one of the most beautiful memories that I cherish in this life. Yet at the same time it was also one of lifes's inevtabe bittersweet noments inasmuch as I wasn't able to be in the extended family gathering that surrounded him at the baptismal font. The problem, I should explain, is that our church has several steps (with no railing) leading up into the Baptismal Font in the chancel and climbing up those steps for me at my age would be a journey much too far and any such attempt would be far more distracting than productive for the congregation. Still, I wanted so much to be a participating part of that moment of heaven's love gathered around the family at the baptismal font. Realizing in my own life my disappointment in not being able to climb a few steps for Xavier's baptismal service, I came to see that there were other services, rites and rituals that are not in common use today such as the presentation of the child during the <u>Feast of Purification</u>, the celebration known as <u>Candlemas</u>,and the <u>Service of Dedication and Presentation</u> of a child which was customary in the time of Anna and Simeon: the <u>Service of Dedication</u> (Luke 2:22f) at which time Joseph offered two turtle doves in the temple as an offering after the birth of Jesus. I have consistently used the service of anointing in our family to remember the baptismal occasion. In the anointing, each child or grandchild is taken up in Grandpa's arms and the child's head is anointed with Grandpa's loving hands. In the 23rd Psalm this anointing was not an honor bestowed but a truth shared and proclaimed. Each year thereafter, our children are reminded of that occasion by our buttering of their noses anew. The picture on the left was taken of Xavier at Betsy's home after dinner I had dipped my fore finger in the salad bowl and anointed him with its oil. If I were translating Scripture today, I would translate "he anointed my head with oil" as better understood to read in our colloquial language as **"I have your back Xavier."** (Psalm 23).

Donald D. McCall

Old Friends Are Best Friends
Matthew 17:1

I was sitting with Barb in our usual pew on Sunday morning when Doug Poland, an Attorney in our church, eased into our pew and put his hand on my shoulder and in a friendly voice said, "May I join you?" It was a brief encounter, but I remember it with pleasure even now because J am not accustomed to being treated with such friendly familiarity by the laity. To be an ordained minister is to be called by God and "Set Apart" during ordination to do whatever God wills for your life. When you are set apart it is very hard to feel as if you are an intimate part of the group. We were taught in Seminary that close friendships will be hard to come by in our parish ministry. In fact, it is still one of the biggest problems among clergy. According to a recent Duke University study "Isolation and loneliness are the two most significant factors in ministerial difficulties and clergy dropout."

Consequently, I felt quite fortunate in being able to clear my calendar on two days in October to have lunch with a couple of 'Old Friends'. We were scheduled to meet John Cochran and his wife on the 6th of October for brunch and Vincent and Molly Carroll on Wednesday the 12th at the Madison Club for lunch. As we looked forward to those dates I told Barbara that I am becoming more and more convinced that old friends are truly the best friends! The years of shared experiences create a bond that transcends the usual and common denominators of friendship. Consequently, you can understand how disappointed I was to receive a phone call from Bette Cochran on the morning of the 6th informing me that John had been taken ill and that they would not be able to meet us for brunch. But Vince and Molly did make it for lunch on the 12th and we had a marvelous time remembering the past and looking forward to what the future might hold. Vincent was the first and the best associate that I ever had at Rochester and he developed the largest youth group that church had ever seen. He was a role model for the young guys and all the gals were madly in love with him. To this day he still exudes that same charisma and I still continue to tease him about it. Barb and I had visited them in Florida and when Vince was the senior chaplain at the US Naval Academy in Annapolis and also when he was stationed in London, England. On Wednesday morning at lunch we picked up the conversation at the very point where we ended it a few years ago. What a marvelous lunch it was. It reminded me of the words of Polonius in Shakespeare's Hamlet (Act I Sc 3)

> "Those friends thou hast, and their adoption tried;
> Grapple them to thy soul with hoops of steel."

As I write this, I am reminded that Jesus had such friends. He had Peter, James and John who shared the intimacy of his friendship. "Jesus took Peter James and John up a high mountain by themselves, and he was transfigured before them." (Matt. 17:1) Again and again we read in scripture that Jesus turned to Peter James and John in the critical moments of His life and I understand now what a difference that friendship made in his life and ministry on earth, because I can now see the positive effects such friendships have made in my life.

I write this to you because I have come to realize that my life has been rich, very rich....not because of anything that I have achieved but rather because of the friendships I have been fortunate to have enjoyed throughout the years. I sincerely hope that you are developing such friendships in your life as you begin your careers.

And thank you Doug, for a friendly pat on the shoulder which started this whole train of thought...

A POSTSCRIPT:

Recently our Church elected a Pastor Nominating Committee to search for a new pastor for our congregation. My wife Barbara was elected as a member of that committee. Driving home from church that day I mentioned to her that considering the enormity of the task they were facing, I felt that there should have been a prayer offered for the committee after they were elected. When we got home that thought was still on my mind, so I sat down and wrote the following prayer which was later published in the **Presbyterian Outlook** magazine (Oct. 2012, pg. 18.)

A PRAYER FOR OUR NEWLY ELECTED PNC

May your first thought be like the last thought
Expressed in the movie Casablanca's final quip;
When Claude Rains says to Bogart at the airport,
"I think this is the beginning of a beautiful friendship."

So, I pray not for a great preacher, priest of saint
I would be happy and welcome without complaint
A pastor who would prove to be a **Friend** for us
A **Friend**...like the "**Friend** we have in Jesus."

Donald D. McCall

$\mathcal{S}$etting Aside Childhood Things
I Corinthians 13

Well, I **sold my Zoom-Zoom!** It was probably the best sports car I ever owned. A two-seater that went so fast that it often got away from me on the road! We traded both the Zoom-Zoom and the PT Cruiser in for a new Chrysler 300 four door sedan. A real old person's luxury car. The front seats are like two leather Barca loungers that are heated for the Wisconsin winters and the radio is a Sirius satellite surround sound which puts you to sleep in the first ten miles! It was a very hard decision for me to make. It marked the end of an era for me. I have had rag-tops since I was in High School.

Pictured here is my Model A with a rumble seat. Seated next to me is my high school sweetheart who is now suffering from Alzheimer's and behind me is Jean Gray whose brother gave the Gray Communications Building to Hastings College. Bob Jacobsen (now deceased) is standing to the rear. The boat that is tied down on top of the car is the first boat I ever made. I designed it as a double kayak and built

Donald D. McCall

it out of scrap lumber and covered it with canvas. It provided hours of fun for us (as you can see) on Crystal Lake. We were young and crazy wild. Now all of that youthful spirit seems gone forever with the selling of my Zoom-Zoom. I tried to express all those feelings to the car dealer but he was too young to understand what I was talking about. But for me it is the end of an era... the end of a long love affair with rag-tops and fast sports cars!

You are probably thinking, "It's about time!" And you are right. It has been a rather extended adolescent period. I thought about that when President Obama gave his inaugural address and said, "In the words of Scripture, the time has come to set aside childish things." Those words from I Cor. 13 reverberated through my mind again when Barb used that chapter as part of her beautiful eulogy for her Father at his funeral service a few weeks ago. Likewise, there comes a time in every life when we have to put aside youthful things and attune our lives to the things of eternal value.

Trading cars was simple. I signed some papers and it was done. Furthermore, the end of an era was not at all painful. And to tell the truth, at my age, I feel better behind the wheel of an old person's car! The real problem that I now face is that I realize that I have some other childish ways that I would like to set aside.

> Like **Selfishness,** a child's trait that I still see cropping up occasionally in my life....

> Like **Anger** that still smolders in my heart....

> Like **Pettiness,** that keeps me from rejoicing with those who rejoice....

> Like **Jealousy**, which sweeps across my mind in hot flashes....

Like **Not Playing Well With Others**, a childish self-centeredness I still need to address....

Like being **Judgmental** ...a hard trait for a minister and former Parole Bd. Chm. to give up....

But selling the Zoom Zoom has given me a new understanding of I **Cor.13:11** and the need to **"set aside childish things."** It was a good lesson in maturity for me to learn, even at my age in life. But more importantly, I have come to realize that the real goal of the Christian Life is to ultimately be able to present oneself as being **"Mature in Christ"** Col.1:28 a goal to which I confess that I must be a *late bloomer!*

$\mathcal{T}$hriving
Ezekiel 17:10

Barbara bought a beautiful lily for us to enjoy during Eastertide.

When it first arrived I thought that it looked a bit scrawny and I doubted that it would survive the trip from the florist shop to our living room. My theological mind, as you might guess, thought instantly of that cliche first popularized in Ezekiels parable of the vine: **"When it is transplanted, will it thrive?** I had succumbed in panic for a moment to the modern fear of the **failure to thrive syndrome.** So wewatered the plant and nourished it and turned it again and again toward the sunlight ... and behold, it's beauty and fragrance soon filled our living room. But my mind remained focused on our modern fear of the possibility of failing to thrive .

Jumping from Ezekiel and the 6th Century BC to the present I too have recently faced the question of **'Thriving".** While I was in the Hospital last month I learned (after peeking at my own medical charts) that the term **'Failure to Thrive'** is also one of the common fears that we face in life's later years. It is a term used in the palliative care of the elderly characterized by unexplained weight loss, and impairment due to some physical disability, which ultimately might bring upon the patient's premature demise.

Then I encountered the term **'Failure to Thrive'** in our local newspaper wherein a journalist was writing about the different test scores of students in different local schools. The article questioned why some students "failed to thrive" in certain districts and if the achievement gaps were due to conditions which needed to be corrected.

For many people the fear of failing to thrive can become a severe and debilitating problem. Or It can become a challenging and growing moment. I remembered that in my midlife years, I sensed the need to do something more...something extra ...something that would add vitality to my daily existence. Life needed to be more than just working and being alive. I was searching for some way to **thrive!** So to activate my mind I started writing down a motivational thought each morning. I discovered that those thoughts gave me a 'jump start' for every day. I found that exercise to be very helpful and realized that it might help others too. I began to hone my thoughts, and when I felt that I had a salable product I bought a half a minute of time during the **TODAY** show on our local NBC-TV every morning at 7:30 a.m. called it _"Today Belongs To You!"_ Then I sold the program to local advertisers. I was **THRIVING** ! It wasn't the money I was making I was making as much as it was the **abundance** of new excitement and creativity that I was experiencing. I loved doing what I was doing.

Following is a 30-second motivational TV spot such as the ones I did ever morning:

> _Good Morning! If Christopher Columbus would have turned back half way into his journey to Discover America, no one would ever have blamed him. But then again no one would ever have remembered him. Success belongs to those who persevere. Today belongs to you. Persevere in everything you do._

Out of that experience came my own personal understanding of what Jesus meant when He said "I **came that you might have life, and have it abundantly!**"(**John 10:10**) Abundantly! That's **THRVING**! Life means more than just being alive. Life was given to us that we might live it abundantly. Living should be thriving! And that abundance is not in quantity but in quality. Not in thriving for the things of this world, but in thriving for the things of the Spirit.... Faith, Hope and Love...and the greatest of these is Love in an abundance of Love. The drive to thrive is the drive to be alive in God's Love and to encourage one another in that Love!

$\mathcal{S}$unday Collection
The Book Of Common Worship

I love the traditions that governed my life when I served in the Navy during the Korean War. Military traditions like family traditions often serve to bond us into a common course of faith and action. **In the olden days** when the Navy was composed of wooden sailing ships, ranking officers would often invite distinguished guests to join them aboard for dinner. Due to the protruding cannons on the ship's side there was no dignified way for guests to board a sailing vessel, when it was at anchor, except by climbing up a rope ladder which was something of a risky feat. It was often necessary for sailors to climb over the side of a ship to reach down and bare an arm, risking life and limb, to assist in pulling the visitor aboard manually. These sailors were called **"Sideboys"**. In the Navy Manual the bosun's call for that exercise was called "Piping the Side". Nowadays "Piping the Side" is a highly formalized Navy ritual with sideboys, who at the order of "**Present Arms**" stand at a modern easily accessible gangway to welcome dignitaries and senior officers coming aboard the ship.

I share all this military nickel knowledge because the remembrance of such occasions on board ship and the sound of the deck officer shouting **"Present Arms"** rings clearly in my memory every Sunday morning at church when it comes time for the morning **OFFERING**. As I hear it, the Liturgist (Deck Officer) stands at the chancel steps

Donald D. McCall

and calls for the "Piping Of The Plates". Then the Ushers (Sideboys) come running down the aisles to assist in bringing aboard our gifts. At the command of **"(Present ALMS")** they stretch their offering plates in front of them and the liturgist whisks them away. It's a mental image that I just can't get out of my mind.

Consequently I am always curious (and a bit anxious) to hear how the liturgist will announce "**THE OFFERING**". St. Paul often asked congregations to contribute to the needs of others as necessary. However, in modern times it sounds almost compulsory as liturgists say, "Let us **receive** the morning offering." implying that a particular Church is the recipient of our gifts. Other liturgists say, "Let us take up the morning **collection**" as if the church were a modern collection agency accepting what is due as payment for the privilege of attending a service of worship. Some say "Let us now bring forth our **Tithes** and offerings" as if a duty tax like a Tithe can possibly express a heart overflowing with love! Nowadays with a Visa card you can you can present your offering without even being present to present it. Every Sunday I go through this moment of wonderment at the time of the "**OFFERING**" which should be the most solemn and sublime moment in the Worship service.

Somewhere and somehow over the centuries we have lost the first reason for an offering,… namely to offer ourselves to God for Love's sake….like a sideboy who scrambles over the ships side to offers his life for others.

*"The Christian life is an offering **of one's self** to God. In worship we are presented with the costly self offering of Jesus Christ. and are led to respond by offering to Him their lives."* (The Directory for Worship; The Book of Order)

That is why at the close of a Service of Holy Communion when we have received the gifts of bread and wine we pray: *"And now we offer and present unto Thee ourselves, our souls and our bodies; to be a reasonable, holy and living sacrifice…of praise and thanksgiving."* (The Book Of Common Worship)

What bothers me the most is the realization that when I was

commissioned by Congress to be an officer in the United States Navy, I raised my hand and took an oath that I was willing to lay down my life for my country.. But when I was ordained as a Presbyterian minister I only had to respond to questions regarding my faith and belief in Christ; in the acceptance of the scriptures; the confessisons; the endorsement of the church's form of government and my willingness to govern myself accordingly. I wish now that I would have been asked if I was willing to lay down my life for Christ's sake…. or at least, like a **sideboy**, to be willing to leap over the side of the ship to assist in that effort.

It's the giving of one's self that Love demands. In James Russell Lowell's poem, that's the lesson that Sir Launfal learned **toward the end of his life** and at the end of his quest for the Holy Grail. He returns to his castle, *"An old bent man, worn out and frail; He came back after seeking the Holy Grail."* At the drawbridge of the castle, he sees a loathsome leper begging alms. Having spent all of his wealth in search of the Holy Grail and having nothing left to give, he dismounts and gives the leper his last crust of moldy bread and water in a wooden bowl. Then the leper is transfigured and he becomes a vision of Christ Himself. A voice, softer than silence, says:

"Lo, it is I, Be not afraid! The Holy supper is kept indeed, In whatsoever we share with another's need.

Not what we give, but what we share; For the gift without the giver is bare;

Who gives himself with his alms feeds three; Himself, his hungering neighbor and Me."

And that is the Lesson that I am learning anew **toward the end of my life:** What is important lies not in what is in the Offering Plate but rather in what lies in our hearts… **presenting ourselves** with our Alms.

Donald D. McCall

$\mathcal{A}$ Fraudulent Illusion
Luke 20:46

I was sitting in church last Sunday and happened to look down at the pew support leg in front of me and I noticed that it was a laminated piece of wood. I rather expected to see a sturdy piece of oak wood supporting the great weight of the overweight person sitting in front of me. I was rather disappointed to see that the cheaper wood used to build the pew had been covered with a veneer laminated to it to make it look sturdier than it really was. There was something disingenuous about it. I thought to myself that if Jesus were here he would probably make a parable out of this situation, telling the people who followed after him not to be like veneered or laminated wood... sturdy looking on the outside but really weak and inferior on the inside. Or don't be like the Pharisees, all decked out in a veneer of fancy robes on the outside but in actuality not very religious in their daily lives.

Thinking those thoughts reminded me of the 19 years that I was in the pulpit at Rochester. I enjoyed them immensely, but I was always torn between being who I wanted to be and who I was 'Called' to be as the senior minister of a large 2000 plus member downtown church. And the following text kept appearing in the forefront of my thinking: "Beware of the scribes, who like to walk around in long robes, and love respectful greetings in the market places, and chief seats in the synagogues and places of honor at banquets (Luke 20:46) can't recall the number of banquets where as the Invocateur I held one of the chief seats of <u>honour</u> on the dais, or the number of places where I was invited in order to add the impression of the church's blessing upon an occasion. Above all else I did not want to be like the ancient Pharisees, living with a <u>veneer</u> of respectability laid upon me! The thing that was so appealing to me about Jesus was his authenticity. He was uniquely who he was.

All of these feelings came simmering to a head one day when I was introduced at some public function as the pulpit voice of the "Prestigious First Presbyterian Church". The word prestigious ricochet like a rocket in my brain sending off sparks in every direction. It occurred to me that I had become what I feared most, a friggin' Pharisee! You see, in its original form prestigious in the Latin language meant "an illusion, a deception, a fraud didn't want be introduced as a sham or as the minister of a church that was a sham!

I wanted desperately to be obedient to my ordination vows. To live the authentic life of Christian discipleship. I remembered so well my father's departing words to nte as I set forth to make my own way in life. Very simply he took me aside, put his hand on my forearm, and quietly, yet very sternly said..."Donald, be yourself." Words similar to the parting advice Polonius gave to Laertes: in Shakespeare's <u>Hamlet</u>: "This above all else, to thine own self be true. And it must follow, as the night and the day that thou canst then be false to no man,"

I now share my Father's advice with you and at the same time I want to tell you how proud I am that you have all been true to your own selves that were so very new and unique when you were born. There was never another like you...and there never will be. I often pause and reflect with amazement at your achievements. And salute you for being who you are, living authentic lives where your true selves shine through!

Let me close with this quote that I recently found among the many notes that I have saved interleaved in my Bible. I hope I've lived by it. "He loved his children, not in order to bind them to himself, but to set them free to be themselves."

Donald D. McCall

$\mathcal{B}$eing A Blessing
Genesis 12:2

When I was a young scholar visiting the Vatican in Rome, I had the opportunity to have an "Audience" with Pope Paul VI. It was an experience that I still cherish to this day; I arrived early at the appointed hour and entered the Papal reception hall. I was soon seated down front by the speaker's platform. In due time a few Cardinals began to arrive and they were seated at the rostrum where they individually greeted the audience and instructed us concerning the proper protocol and procedures for the day. Soon, without any ceremony or fanfare the Pope entered though the great doors in the back of the room. He was seated on a sedan chair being carried on the shoulders of six Swiss guards. We all automatically stood and shouted aloud "El Papa, El Papa". The emotional frenzy was exhilarating and contagious. After a brief homily the Pope gave us his 'Blessing' and it was all over. As I walked out my heart, felt strangely warmed and I realized...perhaps for the first time in my life...how important it is to "Be Blessed" or at least to "Feel Blessed".

Some months later I learned that my closest friend during my Navy years on a Destroyer in the Korean War was going to be consecrated as a Priest in the Catholic Church. Remembering our many escapades while on shore leave in various ports I knew I couldn't miss his ordination service. It was spiritually quite impressive. At the end of the service the new Priests were given special sites in the

Cathedral where they could be greeted by family and friends and pronounce their First Blessings. I was among the first in line to kneel and receive a Blessing from a former Comrade in Arms. On the long drive home I was surprised to feel strangely warmed in heart and I realized that God had imparted His love to me through his newly consecrated priest.

Now the Catholic Church has placed more emphasis on the 'Giving and Receiving of Blessings' than we as Protestants have. However, Martin Luther's Reformation changed all of that. In his Doctrine of the "Priesthood of All Believers", he taught that every Christian has the power to Bless. So while driving home from the ordination service at the Cathedral I remembered how I had emphasized that article of faith in my M Th thesis at Luther Seminary and realized that I needed to implement it more actively in my own life. Upon returning home I decided that before going to bed I would go into the children's bedrooms, ostensibly to make sure that they were all right, but in reality to go in to pronounce a Blessing on each one of them as they slept. I was not surprised that when I returned to my own bed my heart felt strangely warmed and I slept soundly through the night. It became a habit that has lived with me through the years and still lives in my prayers every night.

Biblically, I believe we were born to be blessed. In the first pages of the Bible we read that when "God created humankind in his image..." He then Blessed them. (Genesis 1:27-28) Not to be anthropomorphic, but I'm sure that God's heart was strangely warmed at that moment for God's Blessing was a gift of God's Love....a Father's love... and I know what that feels like.

A few pages later in Genesis God gives us the 2nd Law of Love. God said to Abraham, "I will Bless you." (Genesis 12:2) So it was from the very beginning that we were "Born to Bless" and then in turn we were charged to Become a Blessing to others.

It was at about that time that I realized in my Pulpit Ministry that I needed to change the Liturgy in our Sunday worship service. For well over a hundred years the Sunday Service at Rochester had

concluded with a "Benediction". (A 'bene' Good; 'Dictum' word)
But as I looked out at all those loving faces I realized that they
needed more than a "Good Word" so I began closing worship with
the Aaronic Blessing:

The Lord bless you and keep you; the Lord cause his face to
shine upon you, and be gracious unto you; the Lord lift up his
countenance upon you, and give you peace," Num 6:24-26.

I must tell you that as I stepped down from the chancel steps
after Blessing the congregation my heart felt strangely warmed*

Now let me tell you about one of the darkest days of my life. It
was the day that I had to put my father in a care facility. I cannot
describe the anguish of conscience, the guilt, the despair, the betrayal
that I felt when I consigned him to his shared room. As I was leaving
to drive back to Rochester he surprised me by taking my hand, then
looking upon me lovingly he said, "You've been a good son." It was
my Father's way of Blessing me for the last time. My heart has been
strangely warmed ever since.

All of these thoughts converged in my mind on Thanksgiving
Day when over 20 of us gathered together as extended family at
Betsy's home here in Madison. Just before the turkey was brought
to the table, Betsy invited us all to pause for a moment and share the
"Blazek Blessing" a generational prayer which for years we have all
used at mealtime. It was a quieting moment...a beautiful moment ...
reminding us all that we are all born to Bless and be Blessed. You
could sense we were all strangely warmed. Bless you, Betsy!

$\mathcal{S}$eeking Your Good
Jeremiah 45:4-5

Barb left early in the morning a week ago to Chicago to visit Jen and to see once again the wee baby Lauren. So I decided to drive down to Dickeyville, Wisconsin to see the locally famous Dickeyville Grotto. Every time you drive on Highway #151 you see signs inviting you to stop and see the Grotto erected to honor the Blessed Virgin at the Holy Ghost Catholic church in Dickeyville. Time has never allowed me the opportunity to stop and see the sacred shrine nor visit the gift shop with its complete line of religious gifts and souvenirs. So I took the time to drive down and see it. It was built by Father Wernerus in the years 1925-1930 out of old bottles, glass artifacts and stones from every state in the union and then he cemented the whole thing together without benefit of a blueprint! Today it stands as more of a witness of the spiritual devotion and perseverance on the part of Father Wernerus than of its original intent as a Shrine to the Blessed Virgin!

As I drove home I realized that there were no signs along along Interstate 80 inviting you to turn off at the Rochester exit and see the shrine built to preserve the pulpit where McCall preached for almost 20 years of his life! Many of my boyhood friends all have shrines they have built which bear their names. Mounir Naoum my boyhood friend from Lebanon emigrated to Brazil after the war and now as a multimillionaire business man has built a new Hotel in Brazilia to add to his holdings. Its named the <u>Naoum Plaza</u>. Tom Osborne from Hastings has the new college Stadium and Athletic Complex named after him and the university has named its Football field <u>Osborne Field</u>. College mates <u>Bill Barret</u> and Jim Hazellrig both have buildings on campus named after them. Not much of a shrine, but <u>Bill Madden</u> a Hastings College athlete even has a road named after him! It was a thoughtful though discouraging and soul wrenching drive home as I realized that I have no lasting shrine to commemorate my years of devotion and perseverance and honor for my worldly endeavors.

When I arrived back home I walked into my study and saw my four walls decorated with glass framed honors and degrees and historical memorabilia and I suddenly realized that I had in fact been building my own shrine over the years. Unfortunately it was not to honor the Blessed Virgin...but rather everything on display was there to honor myself. I sit every day cocooned in my own glory. Then it came to me... like a bolt of lightning ...a text that I have never dared to use as a basis for a sermon, but have often thought about. Jeremiah is speaking the Word of God to Baruch, who like me was white haired and had come to the end of his time. Jeremiah the Prophet said, "Baruch, are you seeking some great thing ...some great honor for yourself? Forget it!" (Jeremiah 45:4-5) The life of devotion and discipleship is an altruistic life...<u>a loving life</u> that seeks the good of others and not of ones self. When I was a much younger man, Psalm 122:9 *"I will seek your good"* was my North Star. My intent was to live the altruistic life. But now after reconsidering these texts I see the need to refocus and re-chart my course in life.. .Like Baruch... I'm not too old to re-learn that most important lesson of life that I was reminded of while on a drive home from Dickeyville!

Even now, while writing this letter to you I am reminded of a visit I made to the office of a very prominent U. S. Senator years ago and how amazed I was at the great number of honors and certificates that he had upon his office wall. Later while recounting my visit to Barb, it occurred to me that he didn't have a single picture of his family and children adorning his office walls. I realized later that I had come away with a very negative response to his personal "kingdom building"... his building a shrine to his own glory!

Well, thanks to the Grotto of Dickeyville and a days drive in the countryside, and time to think about my own life, I think I'll now take down all the honors and certificates mounted on my study walls and replace them with pictures of my children and all of you and re-make my study into "A Grotto Seeking and Praying Only For Your Good".

*F*ather, I Have Sinned
Luke 15:21

Toward the end of his life the Dutch artist Rembrandt completed one of the greatest masterpieces of his prodigious career. He entitled it "The Return of The Prodigal Son". In the painting the son returns after years of wasting his inheritance and his life, and kneels before his father in repentance saying, "Father, I have sinned."(Luke 15:21)

Toward the end of his life the Dutch theologian Henri Nouwen traveled to Russia just to see that original work of art. He then wrote a book of the same title which has helped many Christians come to grips with the depth of the pathos associated with the son's confession, as well as one's own personal need to also make such a confession.

Toward the end of my life, more than ever before, it is that same confession of sin that I seek to make when I attend worship services at our church each week. Unfortunately however, confession is not at the heart of our Protestant form of worship today. We associate it with an archaic practice of the Roman Catholic Church where the first words of a penitent in entering the confessional are "Father, I have sinned…".

The closest confession or personal admission of sin by a Protestant is found in the Sunday worship bulletin after the generic corporate 'Prayer of Confession'. The liturgical suggestion for a personal confession of sin offered by the <u>Worshipbook</u> is that at this point in the worship service "*The people may pray silently*" . Our bulletincalls it "*A Moment of Silent Prayer*". That specified moment of silent prayer barely gives one the chance to utter the words, "Father, I have sinned." I find it a great loss that we have not provided in our printed order of worship the time necessary to consider and confess our own deep personal sense of sin and guilt. There is no opportunity in our modern liturgy to approach God with introspection and the words of the Prodigal Son, "Father I have sinned." Somewhere and somehow we have forgone the Priestly function of the ministry which even the early days of the Reformation was still considered to be a vital aspect of the Pastoral role.

In reality, Confession was the prolegomena to hearing the Gospel. It was the cry of John the Baptist who introduced Jesus with the command, "Repent, for the Kingdom of Heaven is at hand." (Mt. 3:2) Repent, Confess, Metanoia,. We are expected to approach Christ as the Prodigal Son approached his Father, in a spirit of contrition. Likewise, we are expected to approach worship in the same manner and that is not something that you can do "in a moment'. We each enter the sanctuary with a burden of guilt and sin that we need to confront and confess.

I remember so well the haunting feeling that I experienced at Seminary when my own sense of sin and prodigal unworthiness gnawed away at the roots of my being. After I graduated from Seminary at Princeton I enrolled for a further degree in Systematic Theology at Luther Seminary in St. Paul, Minnesota. I felt as if I needed to draw water from a different well. There I learned that Luther believed strongly in the confessional, not in a coercive and punitive manner, nor for pecuniary purposes. But rather in a redemptive way. He wanted to change the Confessional from it's abusive use into a therapeutic means of helping us to be cleansed from our sins and to change our ways. Luther laments the fact that since private confession to clergy was no longer mandatory people tended to neglect it. Luther insists that it should be seen as a part

Donald D. McCall

of the priestly function of clergy to help us understand, as did the prodigal son, that confessing one's sin is the first step toward reconciliation and redemption.

As time passed and as I gained some theological maturity I began to realize that I needed someone to whom I could turn to and confess my own growing sense of anguish and inadequacy as a minister. Oh, to be sure, Princeton had served me well and I was at a young age the Head of Staff in a church of over 2000 members with a second book contract in hand, a daily local NBC Television show and a full head of steam for the future. It was then that I realized that my ego was the "Full head of Steam" and though that energy could move an institution forward it couldn't change the direction that my life was taking. I was becoming an institutional leader when all I really wanted to be was a loving follower of my Lord. It hit me one evening like a thunderclap when at a social gathering I overheard one person asking another, "Do you belong to Dr. McCall's Church?". It was an innocent conversational question but it was suddenly a revelation to me. I realized that I had drawn more attention to myself than to the Gospel that I was ordained to proclaim. I had become the very institutional type of leader that I loathed when I was a young student in Seminary. That old sense of prodigal unworthiness, of having wasted my substance began gnawing away at my spiritual roots again.

That night as I was in bed and unable to fall asleep I remembered that when I was a student at the Univ. of Glasgow, Dr Wm. Barclay, in one of our many private conversations, mentioned to me that at morning tea every day I acted more like a politician gathering votes for election to Parliament rather than a serious student of the Gospel. He told me quite frankly that he doubted that I was profiting from his lectures and that maybe I needed to take some time to be, as he said, alone **with God** in order to examine my calling. That was a difficult conversation but at the same time it was a most necessary one...and I am in his debt to this day.

It wasn't many years later, while I was still mulling over Dr.

Barclays's breakthrough conversation that I realized that I still needed more time to be **alone with God.** So I leased a BMW 1000 motorcycle in Germany and drove it over the Alps to Genoa in Italy where I boarded a ship for Tunisia and then drove my motorcycle east to the Algerian border and then down into the Sahara desert there to spend a few weeks motorcycling across the Sahara whilst at the same time being **alone with God.** I had packed a copy of the "Confessions of St. Augustine" in my saddle bag and I read from it daily. Then one morning I came upon these words,

> "O Lord my God, behold and see and have mercy
> and heal me. Thou in whose presence I have become a
> problem to myself; and that is my infirmity." (pg.151)

There it was. The confession I needed to make. I knelt down in the middle of the Sahara Desert in the middle of my life, and using my motorcycle as a prie-dieu, I made my confession. "*I have become a problem to myself*". The relief that came to me was overwhelming.

It wasn't long after that experience that the Governor of Nebraska, who knew of my years of service to the Mayo Clinic as a member of their IRB (Institutional Review Board, which examines the Risk-Benefit ratio of every invasive procedure proposed at Mayo) appointed me to serve on the Nebraska State Board of Parole – a risk benefit decision making body. It was there and then that I became a vocal proponent of the need and necessity of the Confessional. The Criminal Justice system believes that Confession to a crime is the first step toward rehabilitation and consequently I began every Parole Hearing with the following question to the offender, "Are you guilty of this crime?". I was always amazed at the responses. How often an offender would massage the truth to make it appear that they were the victims rather than the perpetrators of a crime. I began to see anew how clearly we do the same thing when we are faced with the challenge to confess our own sins. Our response is often like that of an arch criminal, "Yes. I am guilty...But it really wasn't my fault". I

Donald D. McCall

realized in a new way that we too often massage the truth and offer excuses rather than confessions in our Sunday Morning "Moments of Silent Prayers" to God.

My next question to an offender appearing at a Parole Hearing was, "What have you done to change your behavioral pattern of life?". Confession without an effort to change is simply a liturgical exercise. There must be some evidence of change., such as Jesus gave to a sinner in Galilee, "Go and sin no more." It was while I was serving as Chairman of the Parole Board that I came to a true understanding, as did Martin Luther, of the great need for more than just a moment on Sunday morning for the confession of my sins. There had to be some transforming power taking place within my soul and within the life of every penitent.

Consequently, now in my retirement, I have developed the practice of arriving at the Sanctuary of the church I attend a half hour early on Sunday mornings in order to have time to begin the worship hour with John the Baptist's cry to "Repent." And to approach God in a spirit of contrition and confession of my sin. Like a Parole Board Hearing, I find myself sitting in the offenders place in my pew knowing that I need to verbally confess my sin. For I know that my confession is the first step in my rehabilitation. I sit alone in the middle of our family pew where people passing by will not bother me, and where no one but God can hear my confession. It is my new Sahara Desert. It is my Confessional.

So now as a Priest and as a Penitent,
as a Father and as a son,
as a former Parole Board Chairman and now as one
who seeks mercy,
as a Seminarian who is now an octogenarian,
Donald D. McCall

I am at last beginning to understand Rembrandt's painting and why he completed it toward the end of his life. Truly, as Martin

Luther once said, "The anguish of conscience is the beginning of faith" and the confessional is the place to express that anguish of conscience and to experience, even at my age, a new transformational experience in one's life.

$\mathcal{W}$arming Up The Audience
Luke 8:45

When I was in the Parish, I used to walk into the sanctuary on Sunday mornings, shake hands, and visit with the early attendees. It gave me a feeling of being "In touch" with them and frankly, I drew a certain amount of strength from each one of them. In sports, we called this phenomena **'The home court advantage!'** Having the crowd with you ... being **connected t**o the crowd gives you a definite edge. I can still hear my Father's encouraging shouts urging me on when I was playing ball in High School and College and I know it gave me extra stamina to succeed. I am eternally thankful that throughout my life I was privileged to draw energy and inspiration from the assembling crowds as they gathered for worship. I always feel sorry for the minister who has to spend time filling his water glass and shuffling papers on the lectern and checking the microphone before a worship service begins. That Minister is missing his or her greatest opportunity to intimately connect with his audience... the very people who came to hear him speak. I was always aware of the fact that I drew even more of a sense of the enormity of the challenge of preaching when I joined in prayer with the Choir. Thus, by the time I stepped into the pulpit I was always buoyantly invigorated or inspired and ready to preach...even more so when they had to put folding chairs down the aisles!

There is something about being **connected** and in touch with others that enhances our own lives. Jay **Leno** knows that. Which is why he always shares handshakes and high fives with the front row members of his audience. In a recent interview he said, *"Everybody today texts and e mails, so I feel that it is important to **connect** with people. It is one of my favorite parts of the show."* Have no doubt... he is as energized by them as they are by him! Ask my daughter and she'll tell Kate you... or as you can see for yourself in this photo as she and Jay Leno are both enjoying a laugh together as they warm up the TONIGHT show audience.

So you can see why this is one of the characteristics that I admire so much in the life of **Jesus.** He was never afraid to be **connected** with the crowds. The common people heard him gladly and I have always believed that like Leno, Jesus had a home court advantage when he was with a crowd. Like any public personality, he too at times must have drawn strength and affection in being so intimately connected to them. There is a power shared in the presence of others. When Jesus was in the Garden of Gethsemane he needed time to be alone in prayer... yet he took Peter James and John with him. There is a touch of Divinity in knowing that others are praying with you and for you. I hope that my minister feels that sense of encouragement when he sees me sitting in my same place every Sunday morning !

In fact, Jesus was so in touch with the crowds that he could sense even the slightest jostling or touch that drew strength from Him. When a woman touched him in the hope of healing, he paused and asked, **"Who Touched me?"** (Luke **8:45**) It is· the simple act of sensitivity to others ... in a moment of touching that we still **give** and **receive** from one another.

Donald D. McCall

The personal word or touch before a service is memorably more important than the perfunctory praise a minister hears as the Narthex door after the service. I still remember with appreciation my college English Literature professor, Margaret Lorimer who constantly encouraged me to read more and more of the great literary novels of the world. What I remember most is that when we had to take 'Blue Book' essay tests she would walk up and down the aisle between the row of seats and look over our shoulders to see how we were progressing. I remember the great difficulty I had in trying to express my understanding of some the author's ideas. But as she looked over my work she would put her hand on my shoulder and then give me a small tap of encouragement before moving on. It was the memory of that touch of loving approval that propelled me on even through my graduate years. A 'Touch' can do that!

Touching and **feeling connected** is the shared heartbeat of life. I tell you this because I want to share a secret with you. Sometimes when I wake up in the middle of the dark moments of the night I reach over and put my had on Barb, or I slip my hand under the small of her back... just to reassure myself that she is there. And in touching her I receive strength and courage and hope and love. Love is like that. It still heals and gives new inspiration to life... and in the giving, it also receives because Love is like that.

Minister Appreciation Month

by DONALD D. MCCALL

We once had a minister whom I truly detested
Whose preaching was perhaps his very worst fault;
In fact I thought he should have been arrested
And charged with several counts of verbal assault!

He called us names, like "unrepentant sinners"
And once even said we were like "a brood of vipers"
We often saw him eating and drinking at public dinners
With unclean people like tax collectors and hucksters.

But now we have a minister whom I really admire
Whose sermons are always humorous and brief;
And although we know he's "preaching to the choir"
It has been for us, something of a relief!!!

He tells us that God loves us ever so dearly
That it really doesn't matter what we do or say;
And he says it so convincingly and so sincerely
That I no longer even feel the need to pray!

So tell me now, why is my soul so ill at ease
And why does my mind still wonder and doubt;
And why does my heart have no sense of peace
And why do I feel less fervent and devout???

I think I'd like my old minister back
 For now I've come to realize and sense,
That he was probably right on track
And I was the one so dumb and dense
As to take umbrage and personal offense
At the Gospel's attack against my indifference
And my spiritual and moral indolence!!!

*DONALD D. MCCALL is honorably retired
and lives in Madison, Wisc.*

Donald D. McCall

$\mathcal{D}$enying One's Self
Mark 8:34

When I went off to Seminary years ago, my sister in law Evadne gave me as a présent a small leather bound volume entitled <u>The Imitation of Christ</u> by Thomas A Kempis. This devotional classic written in about the year 1441 became the first volume in my now overcrowded Library... and still one of my favourites ! (As was Eavadne!) In browsing through it the other morning I came upon this phrase 'If thou couldst empty thyself perfectly from all things, Jesus would willingly dwell with thee. ' Which sounded suspiciously to me like a paraphrase of the words of 'If any man would come after me, let him deny himself and take up his cross and follow me." Mark 8:34). I thought about those two phrases for quite some time and then it came to me a few weeks ago in the middle of the night that there is a great difference between denying ones self and emptying oneself. I am not aexicologist, but I do dabble into the exact meaning of a few Greek words that I find to be somewhat ambiguous in the New Testament. Words, which given a different twist, can often give a deeper meaning to the text.

For example: to deny can easily be translated in one's mind to simply mean 'to put off. When I was young I denied myself many things knowing that in time I would be able to acquire or achieve them. What you deny yourself simply becomes a later goal to fulfill. In that light it's not hard to deny oneself When I was an enlisted man in the Navy I denied myself the privilege of going to college and becoming a naval officer and instead I enlisted during the Korean War knowing that later in life I could become an officer and in time I did achieve the rank of Commander in the Navy and additionally was twice named an Admiral in the Nebraska Navy.

When I was young I denied myself the effort of writing a book but by midlife people were lined up in the Mall to have me autograph my second book. When Donny and I were building a small sailboat in the back yard I denied myself the pleasure of a larger keel boat but I knew that in time I would enjoy a 30' Coronado beyond measure! My life has not been about denying but rather about postponing. I always knew that my self-image would some day be fulfilled. Delayed gratification is not denial !

It occurred to me that I have not denied myself anything in life! And thus I came to the conclusion that it was not <u>things</u> that Jesus was talking about. The text more accurately should read: "If any man would come after me let him deny <u>his self-image</u> and take up his cross and follow me." I spent a lifetime fulfilling my own self-image going from a small rural parish to a major pulpit in our denomination and then I woke up in the middle of a nightmare a few weeks ago realizing that I had taken the wrong path for all the 90 years of my life! I have denied myself NOTHING! Now I see that it's not things that we have to deny but our image of ourselves. When Jesus called Peter, James and John while they were mending their fishing nets by the Sea of Galilee...he told them to leave their nets behind and take on a <u>new image</u> of themselves as 'Fishers of Men'. Saul on the road to Damascus accepted a <u>new image</u> of himself as Paul who became an Apostle. The woman at the well who talked to Jesus and confessed her sins went back to her village not as a sinner but with a <u>new image</u> of herself as a redeemed child of God.

I think that this is what Thomas A Kempis was writing about in his book which I'm just beginning to understand today. Denying one's self is not about things. It's about emptying yourself of your own self-image, "so that it is no longer I who live but it is Christ who lives in me." (Gal 2:20)

Donald D. McCall

$\mathcal{D}$iscipleship
Luke 14:33

A few days ago, Barb surprised me at lunch time with the gift of a book that she thought I might enjoy. Enjoy? I devoured it. It was the new 910-page best seller by Pulitzer Prize winner Doris Kearns Goodwin entitled "BULLY PULPIT". It is the historical (over 100 pages of footnotes!) account of the intense friendship between Theodore Roosevelt and William Howard Taft until their friendship ended in their battle for the Presidency in 1912. Fascinating as this book is, what I found to be of greater interest were the many anecdotal stories about the two men that are interspersed throughout its pages. One particular account made me laugh so loud that Barb inquisitively asked me to share it with her: This is what I read:

> "Theodore Roosevelt as a Harvard sophomore in 1878 was never content to sit still and listen. He constantly posed questions in class until finally one professor cut him short saying, "Now look here Roosevelt, let me talk, I'm running this course" (pg. 305)

Barb laughed louder than I did. We both know somebody just like that. At our Church we attend an Adult Education Bible

Class of over 50 members, I admittedly ask too many questions every Sunday morning. I also often get the class off track by my constant expository side bars. I know this and I know that it drives the instructor of the class to the limit of his ot her patience...but the subject matter is so exciting and challenging that I just can't hold back. Barb threatens each week to bring Duct Tape to class to cover my mouth but I remind her in the words of Jesus that If I kept quiet "The very stones would cry out!" (Lk.19:40) In other words, there are some issues in life that are too important not to discuss!

Then I read in the church Newsletter that the course for the class in January would be a study of the Gospel according to Matthew. Ah, Good, I thought. Later I read the title of the course: "Living As Disciples Of Jesus". I was totally taken aback! WOW! I thought, they must have meant, "Living As Followers Of Jesus." That's what I am...a Follower of Jesus. Discipleship, I have learned is not for the faint of heart...and I didn't know anybody in that class that could pass muster as a Disciple. I wondered if I should warn the class at our first meeting of the demands of Discipleship. Here are a few. Jesus said: "None of you can become my Disciple if you do not give up all of your possessions." (Lk 14:33) And also, "Whoever does not hate his father and mother...yes, even life itself cannot be my Disciples" (Lk. 14:26) and "Whoever does not take up his cross daily and follow me cannot be my Disciple" (Lk. 14:27)

Wow! That's a pretty steep learning curve. I don't know anyone in the Adult Bible Study Class that is in the least interested in pursuing that kind of a course of study. Furthermore I wondered if I should warn the class at the outset that Discipleship is not something that you can learn as much as it is based upon a relationship with someone whom you encounter. Which is to say that it is not so much apprehending, as it is being apprehended! Discipleship is not to be found in a four week course but only in a life long relationship. Discipleship is a transformational experience. In which you give up who you are and try to become like the Master whom you are

Donald D. McCall

following. Somehow I didn't think that that was where the class wanted to go. And I thought it wiser not to confront them with the true challenge of discipleship is more than asking, ('What Would Jesus Do?' Better to keep my mouth shut and let the leader who is running the course do the talking although I wondered in my heart if keeping silence wasn't perhaps my lack of courage to speak the truth....or at least a denial of my calling!

Well admittedly I am no disciple. I am a journeyman follower. I no longer wear the collar. I no longer claim a pulpit. My vestments and my robe in the closet, tattered, torn and worn with age and I have found my place to be a wooden pew which I occupy every week as I silently sit and contemplating what it means to follow Christ, I am, at the end of my life in the same place where I was when I was first ordained, on a journey exploring the meaning of Discipleship. And in the words of T. S. Eliot, "The end of all our exploring will be to arrive where we started and know the place for the first time."

But I did want you to know that throughout January as I attended our Adult Bible Study Class I kept my silence. I didn't disrupt the teacher nor did I get the class off track by interjecting all the above thoughts which I have carried in my heart and which I now believe I probably should have shared. Sometimes silence, as St. Peter discovered is in reality an act of denial ... and now ... as I sit by my computer writing this chapter ... I find myself wondering if perhaps that's a rooster I hear crowing in the distance. (Luke 22:59-61)

"The wolf shall dwell with the lamb and the leopard shall lie down with the kid,

And the calf and the lion and the fatling together...

And the suckling child shall play over the hole of the asp...

They shall not hurt or destroy in all my mountain ..."

Isaiah 11:6-9

Donald D. McCall

Thoughts After A Brief Morning Spat
Isiah 11:6-9

Forget the wolf and the lamb lying down side by side
I'd be more content with a minor little miracle;
Perhaps one not unlike what the prophet decried,
Yet one that doesn't sound so profoundly Biblical

I'm more concerned about our life here on the prairie
About our daily silly little flares of ego and tempers;
Whereby we hurt and destroy each other unnecessarily
Through our bumbling blunders in our daily encounters

So forget the wolf and the lamb and the suckling child,
For the real test in life for us on earth is this…
To lie down together at each days end …. reconciled
While learning to live together in peaceful bliss!!

Donald D. McCall

$\mathcal{L}$istening As An Act Of Love
Matthew 11:15

The other night I watched the movie "Hemmingway and Gellhorn" a 2012 HBO production that capsules the relationship between Hemmingway and Gellhom during the Spanish Civil War when they were both war correspondents and both living on the same floor in the same hotel. She later became his third wife and inspired him to write the novel "For Whom the Bell Tolls". Likewise, Hemmingway's novels have always inspired me in one way or another, which is why I went to Cuba in 1981 to visit his home and the Havana which he enjoyed so much and which I was enjoying presently because I was gaining new insights into his life. I sat on his veranda for a long time, looking out over the pool and down the hill to the ocean below wondering how anyone could take time to write while living in such a distractingly beautiful setting.

At lunchtime the next day, I pulled Carlos Baker's biography of Hemmingway off a bookshelf and perused it while I was eating my daily grilled cheese sandwich. That 700-page volume is probably the most authoritative biography of Hemmingway ever written and I have underlined more passages in it than I have earmarked in all of the Pentateuch! It was while I was reaching for a few chips that I came across these words that I had underlined years ago which reflected Hemmingway's view of another writers current lack of productivity: "He (the other writer) had stopped listening long ago...

Donald D. McCall

this is what dries a writer up. The minute he starts listening again he will sprout like dry grass after a sizzling rain." (sic)

That thought stayed with me for some time. I realized that if the first duty of a writer is to listen it should then also be true that the first duty of a minister is to listen! I mentioned that to Barb who is on the Pastor Nominating Committee of our church and suggested that though they are looking for a great preacher I hope that the person they choose will also be a great listener. Jesus was a great listener. He sat for a long while and listened to the woman at the well as she unfolded her whole life story. He listened late into the night to Nicodemus as he unloaded some of his theological questions about life and death. He listened to the scribes and the Pharisees as they argued the fine points of their faith with him. He listened to the Centurion from Capernaum and was so impressed with what the man said that he healed the man's daughter instantly. He listened intently to the answer that Peter gave to the question. It is no wonder that he stressed the importance of listening by saying, "He who ears to hear, let him (listen) here!"

When I was a student at Princeton, Barth, Brunner and Bultman were the revered theologians of the world. But I found myself drawn to Paul Tillich who was on the faculty. The first few years of preaching, I realized that I was quoting Tillich more than any of the other theologians including Calvin! I still remember well one of his quotes that I probably used too often but still appreciate to this day and which has quickly come back to mind. It was Tillich who once said: "The first duty of Love is to Listen!"

I feel that Hemmingway, Jesus and Tillich have all recently reminded me of a truth that I have long known and believe to be the rock bottom basis of a happy marriage. The first duty of Love is to Listen! When you truly listen to someone you never get tired of being with th m. When Barb and I lived in Lincoln we would often drive to Omaha to have dinner or to see a movie. Not that the restaurants were any better or the theaters more modern, but rather it was because we enjoyed the o hour drive where we could talk and listen to each other without interruption of any kind for it is in listening that we are drawn closer and closer together.

All of this has come to my mind now as I write this letter to you because the other evening Barb said, "What would you say to driving up to Sturgeon Bay for the weekend?" I am aware of the fact that it's not Sturgeon Bay but that she's looking forward to. I know this for a fact. So, young as all of you are.. and believe this aged friend: "Listening is an act of Love!"

Donald D. McCall

*J*onah's Beach
Matthew 10:42

A NEW YEAR! A Fresh Start! A New Beginning! But with it let me also remind you of the words of the philosopher George Santayana.... words engraved at the entrance of Auschwitz: *"Those who cannot remember the past are condemned to repeat it.".* Thus on New Year's Day I always realize that remembering the past may be just as important as looking hopefully toward the future. In my life I am constantly thankful for the privilege of having been born and raised in Lebanon, the land where Jesus trod and that experience from my past has given me an existential understanding of the Gospels for which I find new inspiration every time I open my Bible.

When I was a boy, my father was the Headmaster of a Presbyterian Mission School in Tripoli, Lebanon. We would often travel south to **Sidon** to visit with the headmaster of the Mission school in that city. While the adults visited my brother and I along with Charlie and Emylou White would all dash down to **Jonah's Beach** to play and swim. It was a beautiful beach, not as salty as the Atlantic Ocean and having only minimal tides. It's seven miles of sandy shore line was acclaimed to be the finest swimming beach on the Eastern Mediterranean shore. Historically, It claimed it's fame as being the beach where the whale had "**spewed out Jonah on the dry land.**" (**Jonah 2:10**) As a boy I believed that account to be true as surely as American children believe that the Puritans landed exactly at Plymouth rock.

Furthermore, for me **Sidon** was a treasure trove of **Biblical lore.** The city itself was named for Sidon, the grandson of Noah. That goes back a long way! The prophet Elijah had performed miracles in Sidon and for that it was later referred to as 'a place of healing'. Jezebel, who later married King Ahab, grew up as a princess in Sidon (and that's how I always envisioned her namesakes at the beach!) **Jesus** preached in Sidon although there is no record of what he said. Matthew records that Jesus did heal a Canaanite woman's daughter at Sidon although there is no Holy Site in that city to commemorate that event. I especially loved playing on **Jonah's Beach** knowing that Jesus and his disciples must have spent more than one warm afternoon relaxing on that same shoreline where I was playing. Jesus also had his memories of Sidon. After leaving Sidon and traveling south to Galilee Jesus referred to those who were following him as "**an evil generation seeking the sign of Jonah."** **(Luke 11:29-32).,** I doubt that many people (if any) in the church I attend even know what the "Sign of Jonah" is but I am sure that memories of Jonah's beach ran through His mind as he issued that warning to the multitudes in Galilee who demanded evidence of

Donald D. McCall

His Messiahship. Which makes me especially appreciative of my childhood convictions of things seen as well as evidence of things unseen but accepted through local historical traditions.

I need to add that more than an intimacy with 'Biblical Lore' I was also privileged to have obtained an **intimacy with the language** and the nuances and customs of life in that ancient country. My mind carries a childhood imagery of many texts not emphasized in the English Versions. When you read the words of Jesus **"whoever gives to one of these little ones, even a cup of cold water to drink, truly I say to you, he shall not lose his reward." (Matt 10:42)** You probably immediately think of the analogy of serving others; caring for others; of being doers and not just hearers of the word. Furthermore, you probably realize that in serving others you are also serving Christ. Those are all worthy thoughts and meaningful interpretations of the text.

But my mind works differently. When I read the text it's not the acting or doing or serving that grabs my attention. It's the word **'COLD'** that jumps out at me. **Cold** water was a luxurious treat in those days before refrigeration and electricity. City water was available through springs, rivers, cisterns, pools, reservoirs and aqueducts. Cold water was best drawn early in the morning from deep wells and then kept in clay pots in a dark place to keep the water cool throughout the day. **Cold** Water was reserved for 'special guests'… those whom we loved, cherished and honored. I remember as a child that my mother would give us a clay jar filled with **COLD** water when we would go out to play….not tap water, but **COLD** water from the fridge….reminding me that I was a child of privilege. But Jesus was telling his disciples to *"give their best"* even to the least deserving …the little children…. In other words he is telling us *"to give our very best"* no matter what and without considering the merit or worthiness of those who receive what we give them. I often think about that when I walk down the hallway of our church and look at the collection barrels awaiting our deposits of "Left-over" clothing for the 'poor'. One time I sensed that the Jesus of my childhood was walking next to me, and sensing that the barrel was for our <u>used</u> clothing, He stopped and took out a blue felt tipped pen and wrote on the barrel, **"My Best for God's Blest"** I still see those words on those barrels to this day!

Living In The Moment
Matthew 6:25-34

Epiphany is the 12ᵗʰ day of Christmas and it celebrates the visit of the Magi to the manger scene in Bethlehem thus *'revealing'* the Incarnation of the Christ child to the whole world. The word *"epiphany'* comes from experience which allows one to understand a problem or situation the Greek (ἐπιφάνεια) meaning *"to reveal, or to suddenly appear"*. In philosophy it refers to any enlightened in a newer or deeper revelation than previously perceived.

Let me share an **Epiphany Moment** that came upon me last month as I was thinking about using a quote from W.H. Auden's classic poem a "Christmas Oratorio". It is the account of the journey of the Wise Men and it tells why each Wise Man followed the Star to Bethlehem. One followed to learn 'To be Truthful **now.**" Another followed to learn "To be Loving **now.**" The third wise man followed the star "To learn to be Living **now.**" Then they all chimed in together and said that they were all seeking "To learn how to be Human **now.**" Well, those are all important virtues to learn and to seek after, and like the Magi we too should be adopting them in our own lives. But then, a few days ago I had an **Epiphany**. A deeper understanding of the poem came to me. The operative words of the poem were not descriptive about the quality of life but rather repeatedly in the form of a directive. The poem was not about how to live but rather about when to live. The operative word of the poem I suddenly realized was now…**Now**…**Now**! The poem was a challenge to live **NOW**..or as we say, "**To Live In The Moment**"

My **Epiphanic Moment** was enhanced recently by the release of the movie "**ALL IS LOST**" starring Robert Redford. It's a movie about an old man sailing alone in the Indian Ocean (you can see why I love it!) His sailboat crashes into a rogue-floating container, which had fallen off a freighter. The container smashes a hole in his yacht and he immediately has to focus all of his attention and energy on surviving the mishap. Not only does he have dozens of minor equipment challenges but he also runs out of water, faces fierce rainstorms and personal fatigue. The point that the movie makes is that Redford has to put out of mind all of his future plans and focus every ounce of his energy on **living in the present moment** which in truth makes this movie a morality lesson on how we ought to live our own lives every day. Survival depends upon how we deal with our present moments in life, not with the future or the past. Living in the present has long been known to be the pathway toward peace in one's life.

That is what Jesus teaches us. After a long discourse on **Learning how to live in the Moment, (Matthew 6:25-34)** He summarizes his disciples with these words, "**Do not worry about tomorrow, for tomorrow will bring worries of its own. Today's trouble is enough for today.**" That's called learning "**How To Live In The Moment.**" I remember discussing that text many years ago with my dear friend John Cochran, former CEO of Firstmerit. It was a long and soul-searching conversation inasmuch as we were both young then and searching for direction in our lives. John, good financial advisor that he was, tried to convince me of the need to save for the future, and I, young idealist that I was tried to convince him of the importance of **Living in the Moment.** A few days later, I received a package from John. It was a heavy bronze Piggy Bank with the following engraving (which you can still almost read) "*To: Pastor Don From: Banker John: "Tucka Buck Away A Day*". I loved it. In fact it's still on my bookshelf even though it's still empty! The only

Donald D. McCall

thing I've saved over the years are the wonderful memories of all the great **Moments in Life** that John and I have shared and which I keep *tucked away* in my heart.

Let me share another **Epiphany Moment** with you. On a recent Sunday morning, we were in Church sitting with Grandchildren in our usual pew. There is a reason that churches have pews instead of chairs. Chairs separate people. Pews allow people to sit closer together. I love sitting every week in our pew next to Barb. Our shoulders touch. Our hips touch. Our thighs touch. And during the prayers our hands touch as we hold each other in prayer. That morning Claire was sitting at Barb's other side, and noticing that we were holding hands in prayer, she gently reached over and placed her hand on top of ours. It was an **Epihany** moment for Claire. She had gone from a childhood understanding of *folding* her hands in prayer to a more mature understanding of the joy of *holding* hands with another in prayer. ....and as for me... I was overjoyed to be **"Living in that moment."**

$\mathcal{V}$anity Of Vanities
Ecclesiastes 1:1-10

Daughter Karen called me from Minneapolis the other night to tell me that she had attended the funeral of an old family friend in Rochester that afternoon. After chatting with her for a while, I asked my usual question: "What text did the minister use at the funeral?" She answered, "It was the first 11 verses of **Ecclesiastes,** But don't ask me why!". I immediately went to my Bible and read Ecclesiastes 1 :1-11.

> *"Vanity of Vanities! All life is vanity. A generation goes and a generation comes. The sun rises; and the sun sets... All things are wearisome ... What has been is what will be...The people o f long ago are not remembered, nor will there be any remembrance of the people yet to come."*

I thought what a bummer of a sermon. I would have chosen Chapter 3:1 which is often used as a classic Old Testament reading at a funeral service: *"For everything there is a season and o time for every matter under the sun; a time to be born, a time to die..."* I have never used Ecclesiastes as a basis for a doctrinal sermon but I have found it to be a textual treasure trove for private meditation and contemplation. I have spent hours sitting on our third-floor deck

Donald D. McCall

looking out over the Wisconsin prairie slowly reading one verse at a time. The title of the book, **"Ecclesiastes"** is a transliteration of the Hebrew word "Kohelet" which means 'Teacher' or 'Wise Sage'.

I read it with the feeling that my father (a college professor) is sitting next to me nudging me at the end of every verse. It's message has inspired some of the world's greatest authors: **Tolstoy's** "A Confession"; **Shakespeare's** Sonnet 59: ("nothing new under the sun"); **Hemmingway's** title for his first book: "The Sun Also Rises"; **Tom Wolfe** whose 1987 novel "The Bonfire Of The Vanities" was a best seller in my pulpit days.

Wolfe wrote:

"Ecclesiastes is the greatest single piece of writing I have ever known and its wisdom expressed is the most Lasting and profound." I too have found that to be true and following are a few of my favourite verses from Ecclesiastes for you to think about and to enjoy.

3:9 "Two are better than one, for if they fall one will lift up the other." Barb and I made this our mental mantra when we were climbing Mt. Fuji in Japan. The wet path up the mountain forced us to hang on to each other to keep from constantly slipping and falling. I still consider lifting one who is falling or one who simply needs 'a lift in life' to be one of the foundation pillars of any relationship.

7:8 "Better is the end of a thing than it's beginning." Now, toward the end of my life, I've learned to enjoy the peace and fulfillment that comes when you no longer are driven by ambition and envy of other people's successes ....for what Ecclesiastes (The Teacher) calls the 'vanity of youthful desires in chasing the wind.

10:8 "Whoever digs a pit (creates a trap) will fall into it." I read a poem years ago by Rev. Lonnquist of the Bethphage Mission in Nebraska, which goes something like this:

"It's one thing to dig a pit;
It's another thing to try to clamber out of it". I

It's a visual truth I've never forgotten, and which still crosses my mind almost daily.

10:18 "SLOTH" the kind of admonition you can take lightly and which I have added to my collection of *Poetic Photos* which I have reproduced for you in this volume.

11:4 "Whoever observes the wind will not sow." I know this refers to those who are waiting for the right moment to begin a task or do a chore... but it also refers to those of us who simply like to sit and look up at the clouds and think and contemplate and day dream.

11:9 "Follow the inclination of your heart, and the desires of your eyes:" (Dream!) This is the text that I would use if Hastings College would invite me back to deliver a record <u>third</u> Baccalaureate sermon! It's a text that really needs to be heard!

12:12 " Of the making of many books there is no end" True... but I will always be eternally grateful for the book that Ecclesiastes has written. Tuck a copy under your pillow some night and give thanks to God for the wonderful life that we have been given to live! You will love, enjoy, cherish and long remember what you've learned!

And By the Bye, this month I celebrate another Birthday. I've already received a birthday card from my mentor Ecclesiastes. On the inside of the birthday card he wrote this memorable salutatory greeting: **"A living dog** is **better than a dead lion."** (Eccl. 9:4)

Donald D. McCall

*E*ncouraging One Another
Colossians 2:2

One of the luxuries that I enjoy in this life is the indoor swimming pool that we have in our home. It's on the ground floor and surrounded by floor to ceiling windows which almost makes you feel that you are outdoors. It's much easier to maintain than an outdoor pool and available for use year round and in any kind of weather. We keep a lot of plastic plants in the pool area for decorative purposes. They need no care. They shed no leaves. Neither are they affected by the accidental abuse of children running wild.

The main part of our home is built around and open Atrium with a glass ceiling which gives you the feeling that you are living outdoors throughout the year while at the same time you are protected from the elements. The grandchildren love to sleep in the Atrium inasmuch as it gives them the opportunity to look up at the stars in the sky when they have to go to bed at night.

I tell you all of this as a prolegomena and explanation of an annual 'discussion' my wife and I have every year. At this time. In the winter time I always take a few of he plastic plants from the pool area and place them in the Atrium. My wife thinks this is a fool's errand. My thinking is that in movg them to the Atrium they will serves as '**encouragement**' for the real plants in the Atrium which always have a hard time surviving the severe Nebraska winters when snow covers the Atrium's glass roof and the plants don't get all the sunlight that they need. So I place the plastic plants alongside the real plants so that the real plants will strive to be as green and as colorful as the plastic ones. Don't laugh! I've done this for years and it works. The real plants thrive when they are surrounded by such encouragement. Let me tell you, encouragement is one of the most powerful gifts that we can give to others.

The apostle Paul knew the importance of that gift of encouragement because he had been the recipient of that gift himself. After his conversion experience few Christians in Jerusalem wanted anything to do with him. They all still feared him except for a man named Barnabas, whose name translated from the Greek means 'Son of Encouragement'. Barnabas was a young convert who sold a field that he owned and gave the money to the Apostles (Acts 4:36f). He vouched for Paul and encouraged Paul to join him on a Missionary journey. Thus Paul was welcomed into the fellowship of the church and with the encouragement of Barnabas Paul became the greatest Missionary ever known to Christendom. Therefore it is easy to understand why Paul always urged the recipients of his letters to always "**encourage one another as your hearts are knit together in Love.**"(Col.2:2)

I too have had a Barnabas in my life in the person of Dr Silas G. Kessler who was the Moderator of the General Assembly of the Presbyterian Church USA in 1963. More than that he was the pastor that confirmed me in the faith, ordained me and encouraged me throughout my life. His letters to me in the course of my ministry were as forceful as St. Paul's letters were to the early church, and they always contained a word of **encouragement!** In the picture to the left you can see that his imprint upon my life was so strong that now, in our later years, we are even beginning to look alike! The truth is that I have become the "**Son**" **of his encouragement.**

Equally important, and the point that I want to make in this chapter is that I want to thank my children for all the encouragement that they have given me in the years gone by. We all too often think of parents encouraging their children, but let me tell you I have learned

Donald D. McCall

that more often than not it's the other way around. My children have been as great if not the greatest source of encouragement in my life simply through their unconstrained confidence in what they believe their parents can do. My children looked upon me as though I possessed an almost magical ability or quality that to them seemed super-human. I know that because that's the way I envisioned my Father when I was a child. And that feeling lasted a lifetime, so it is with most children.

For example: I remember when I decided to motorcycle across the Sahara Desert in North Africa, every one thought that I was out of my mind except my Son Donald Jr. who went out an bought me a very expensive leather jacket for my safety and gave it to me with his **encouragement** to have a great trip!

I remember stopping at a café in Albert Lea Minnesota with my daughter Kate at which time she gave me a few verbal nudges **encouraging** me to think about modifying my life style….for which I thank her to this day.

I remember some very thoughtful conversation with my son Russell when I was visiting him in Australia where he was playing professional basketball and with his **encouragement** I was able to face what was then a very unknown future in my life.

And Karen, my first born, whose middle name is 'Encouragement' who has always been the first to sign on no matter how wild my ideas have been.

I have come to the conclusion that it is **because of such encouragement that our hearts become knit together in love.** That encouragement is one of the strongest forces of love that we are able to give to others in this life.

$\mathcal{H}$ow Prison Changed My Preaching

How prison changed my preaching

BY DONALD D. MCCALL

It was my privilege in the course of my pulpit ministry to be invited by the Mayo Clinic to serve as the public member of their Institution Review Board. The IRB met each week at the clinic. A dozen physicians and I along with the clinic's legal counsel discussed the risk/benefit ratio of every invasive protocol submitted for review. Our discussions were often not only academic inquiries but also times of soulful introspection.

It was because of that background experience that the governor of Nebraska later asked me to serve on the Nebraska Board of Parole — a risk/benefit decision-making board. As my retirement years were approaching, I accepted the appointment with all the excitement of experiencing a new 'Call.' However, I had no inkling of the profound change that my new prison experience would have over my old theological underpinnings, and consequently over my future preaching.

Like delayed post-traumatic stress syndrome, it all flashed back to me last Sunday during our monthly Communion service.

My wife, who is an elder, was serving and therefore I was alone in our customary pew. Having administered the sacrament for over 50 years, I'll admit that I wandered off mentally for a moment or two, but when I focused on the bulletin again, I wondered to myself, "Whatever happened to confession during Communion?" Oh, yes, there was a printed paragraph of Confession at the earlier part of the service. But it certainly didn't leave me sitting there under a deep conviction of sin. Shouldn't I be experiencing a new sense of pardon ... of my sins being expunged?

My post-traumatic mind raced back to my parole board days. I remember receiving a letter from a man who was requesting that the parole board recommend him for a hearing before the board of pardons (composed of the governor, the attorney general and the secretary of state). Parole boards can parole but only the pardon board can grant a pardon ... and frankly they are rarely granted. But this man's letter had a haunting phrase in it that kept coming back to my mind. He was quite old and wanted a pardon so he could meet his savior "not as a convicted felon" but as a man worthy of the life he had been given to live in this world.

In the next few days I researched his file. He was convicted for murder. I almost quit researching right there. Murderers are rarely pardoned. He had been sentenced to life in prison in 1956. In 1970 his sentence was commuted to a term of 25-45 years. I kept on reading. He had done the time required by his sentencing judge and had an excellent prison record with many commendations. Years later he was paroled to another state where he became a groundskeeper for the state, and later he was promoted to head groundskeeper.

> The old man sat before the board of pardons. When the governor announced its decision, there was a moment of hushed silence. Then a small outburst of praise to God that had been building up within him for over 30 years, "Thank God."

He remarried. He became a member of Kiwanis, a Presbyterian elder, a benefactor to society, and he hadn't even received as much as a parking meter violation in the more than 20 years he had been out of prison. In our correspondence, I grew more and more in my admiration of what he had achieved in life since his parole. We unanimously recommended him for a hearing before the board of pardons.

When the day of his hearing before the pardon board arrived, a large crowd had gathered in the governor's hearing room. Television cameras from several stations were lined up against the north wall, and there was only standing room left for the many who came to support him. He sat at a small table in front of the board. They were sitting on a raised dais. Even I was a bit intimidated by the power represented by the three members of the pardons board.

The governor convened the hearing. He asked

76

Donald D. McCall

From *The Presbyterian Outlook*
September 19, 2011

$\mathcal{G}$ adara
Mark 5:1-20

There are some things...some people...some places that you just love instinctively. When we bought our house in Lincoln, NE. over **30** years ago I said to the Realtor as we entered it, **"This is it. This is where I want to live until I die!"**. The house had a **glass-roofed atrium** at its center and a glass-enclosed pool on its south side. A double driveway provided us with a perfect basketball court. It was a preacher's perfect hideaway. Then when we moved to Madison **10** years ago to be nearer the children and the grandchildren we also moved our membership to Covenant church. On the first Sunday that I walked into Covenant's doors I turned to Barb and said, **"This is it. This is where I want to attend church until the day I die."** (A comment that had a familiar ring to it, but which now seems more imminent than it did **30** years ago) I love this church...its ministers and staff....its loving spirit....its theological heritage and especially that circle of friends who sit within arm's reach of me every Sunday morning and whom I consider to be my extended family.

However...now that I think of it, there is one thing that bothers me and it has bothered me since that day I entered through the front doors. The first thing that you see as you walk into Covenant church is a large framed poster in the Narthex which urges you to immediately leave and **"Go therefore and make disciples of all nations." (Mattt. 28:19).** Instead of inviting me in to share life with

Donald D. McCall

you it encouraged me to leave and to go carry the gospel somewhere else in the world. That's not a particularly welcoming sign. I came here because **its where I want to live until I die** and the first thing you ask me to do is to leave and go elsewhere. I've sat in my pew on many Sundays thinking of donating a new sign with a more inviting imagery Something like a shepherd watching over his sheep; or a picture of Christ with his arms open saying "Come unto me…"; or a painting of a stream in the meadows and the words, "Come ye apart and rest awhile". Anything would be better than a poster telling me to 'Go Elsewhere'.

I substantiate my thinking by referring to the one account in Scripture where Jesus rejected the request of a healed man who wanted to follow him. Instead, Jesus instructed him to stay where he was and bloom where he was planted!

It happened when Jesus was preaching in the hill country of **Gadara**. A man who was demon possessed begged Jesus for healing. Then Jesus noticing a herd of swine nearby cast the demons out of the man and into a herd of swine about 2000 of them who then came crashing down from the step banks of the cliffs and into the sea where they drowned. (Mark 5:1-20) When news of this miracle spread, the townspeople came out to see what it was that had happened. And they saw Jesus and the former demoniac sitting there at His feet and clothed and in his right mind. Later when Jesus was getting into his boat to leave, the man who had been possessed with demons came to him and begged him that he might also go with them. **"But Jesus refused him and said, 'Go home to your friends and tell them how much the Lord has done for you'. And the man went and began to proclaim about how much Jesus had done for him. And every one was amazed."**

I love that Gospel story. Unlike the huge poster in our Narthex, **Jesus is telling us to stay where we are.** We don't have to go to distant lands to see miracles performed. Stay at home and tell your friends how Jesus has changed your life and you will see miracles all around you day by day. This is an inviting story where Jesus invites us into ministry right where we are. And it works. Later in Marks Gospel **(Mark 7:31 and 8:1-10)** we read that Jess was revisiting in the region of **Gadara** and a great crowd numbering over 4000 people had gathered to hear him. It's called the "Feeding of the 4000" **(Mark 8:9)** many of whom were there because Jesus told a healed demoniac to stay close to home and "**proclaim how much Jesus had done for him.**"

I think we need to hang the picture of "The Cliffs of Gadara" in our Narthex to remind us that there are miracles to be wrought right here at Covenant Church if we will proclaim how much Jesus has done for us. I'm thinking now of the need to build a **glass covered atrium** over the garden area between the Sanctuary and the Education Unit to accommodate the future crowds that will gather to hear the Gospel proclaimed here at Covenant. I've even gone so far as to consider a name for that atrium gathering space: "The Gadarene Room"

Donald D. McCall

Old School Ties
Luke 2

Christmas was always such a miraculous celebration at church. Cookies showed up daily at the church office. Meetings were by their own nature gradually transformed into yuletide celebrations. There was always the scent of candles burning and the fragrance of recently cut pine boughs decorating the chancel and lining the sills of the stained glass windows in the sanctuary. Life at the church seemed miraculously changed. More than an annual celebration, it became a constantly new **encounter** with the celebration of the birth of Jesus at Bethlehem.

I share all of this because I want to tell you about my Christmas at Rochester in 1985. I had lunch one day in early December at the University Club in the Kahler Hotel and happened to **encounter** a close physician friend who confided in me that a patient of his named Dr. Charles Malik, of Lebanon and former President of the United Nations Assembly was coming to Mayo's for surgery. Since I was born in Lebanon, he wondered if I knew him. I said, "Know him? We went to the same school." (My Father was the Headmaster of Tripoli Boys School, a Presbyterian Mission School in Northern Lebanon.) Then I asked my friend to make arrangements for me to meet Dr. Malik's flight at the airport in order to save him the hassle of getting to his hotel…a common courtesy for many dignitaries. A few days later when his flight arrived I was standing in the airport receiving area waiting for him to disembark. Dr. Malik is a tall man, an inch taller than I am with another inch of well-coifed white hair. You couldn't miss him…not even in a crowded airport. I walked right up to him and stood face to face in front of him while bobbing my head around him as if looking for someone. He responded in kind. Then I quietly began to whistle our old school song: *"A song of songs for the school on the hill"*. Memories of his childhood flashed through his mind as he listened and looked at me. I said "Donald McCall". He blinked and then blurted out the word "Dawnie". It was an **encounter** of pure joy. (We had last met in 1965 when he was a guest in my Father's home Dr. Malik at the UN at Hastings College) We embraced with tears and laughter and then I took him and his wife to their hotel and made all the arrangements necessary for their comfort and convenience during their Rochester stay.

Now, every year at Christmas time the Mayo Clinic presents a Community Wide Christmas Celebration at the Civic Auditorium. It was something like an expanded family "Evening of Caroling" with the Scriptures read and felicitations expressed. It was all"In House" and presented by the Mayo Staff. I asked the Board of Governors if this year, as an exception, they would consider asking Dr. Malik to read the Scriptures. It was always from Luke 2. They thought it was a splendid idea. He had a PhD in metaphysics from Harvard, studied Theology under Heidegger in Germany. Taught at Notre Dame, Dartmouth and other international Universities. Furthermore, Dr. Malik has received a world record of **68** Honorary Degrees (yes… **68!**) and was the past president of the United Nations General Assembly. His books on Human Rights and Christian Culture were internationally published. My favorite was entitled <u>*"Man in The Struggle For Peace"*</u> which I have with his autograph and resting now on that special shelf in my library.

I picked up Dr. and Mrs. Malik on the evening of the Christmas Event and after we arrived at the City Auditorium he chose <u>not</u> to sit on the stage with the other dignitaries and presenters but rather to sit in the front row of the main floor with his wife. (I loved him

Donald D. McCall

for that!) When it was time for him to read the Scriptures I helped him up to the steps of the proscenium of the stage. After placing his Bible on the lectern he looked out over the audience, scanning it as if he were looking out over the shepherd's fields of Bethlehem. Then he read from Luke 2 until he came to the passage **"Now in that country there were shepherds keeping watch over their flocks by night…"**

At that point he paused, took off his glasses, looked up from his Bible and said, "That country is my country." and he began to describe the manger scene in such a personal way that we all felt that we too were **encountering** the birth of Jesus for the first time in our lives. You could hear a pin drop…our hearts were greatly moved….he was investing himself in the text….and we were too. I still remember one of Dr. Malik's most memorable quotes:

> *"The greatest thing about any civilization is the human person, and the greatest thing about this person is the possibility of his encounter with the person of Jesus Christ."*

The memory of those words and of that evening will be forever with me.

A few days later, I was in Dr. Malik's hospital room as they were ready to take him to surgery. As we went down the hall, he reached out his hand from his gurney. I took it in mine. It was larger than mine. After a few minutes, I realized that I was not the only one at his side. Another hand… a strong hand had reached through the other side of the gurney and grasped Dr. Malik's left hand. I recognized that carpenter's hand immediately…the deep print of a large nail was still visible….I knew who **He** was…but I was too intimidated to look up into **His** face. All I remember from that **encounter** was that at that moment I felt a sudden sense of calm and deep peace in my life. It's that same sense of Calm and Peace which I now wish for you this year as we approach the celebration of Christmas.

$\mathcal{K}$eeping One's Silence
Luke 19:40

One of my most pleasurable memories of the many years we lived in Lincoln was in looking forward to dinner time each evening. Everyone had something to say. And it was always something we hadn't heard before! Then after dinner the boys would be off to the races and Barb, Jen, Betsy and I would linger over coffee and discuss whatever issue of the day that we found interesting, arguable, ;or debatable. You probably wonder what chance a theologian had debating with three burgeoning lawyers. So did I. but it was always great fun and as challenging as king Solomon predicted in Proverbs 27:17 "As iron sharpens iron, so one person sharpens the mind of another." I always thought that Barb should needlepoint that text and frame it to hang on our dining room wall. I will admit, however, that their arguments and logical thinking often a gave me new insights into the necessity of speaking truth to power as did Jesus when responding to civil authorities when they demanded that his disciples and followers who were waving palm branches as they paraded through the Golden Gate into Jerusalem. Jesus said, "If my disciples and followers kept their silence the very stones would cry out." (Luke 19:40) In those dinner time conversations I learned that there are times when you just have to speak t against social injustice. It may not change the injustice you are decrying, but it will change you!

Again, as chairman of the Parole Board I have to admit that

Donald D. McCall

my speaking out against prison injustices didn't change much of anything - except that it gave the editorial cartoonist for the Omaha World Herald multiple chances to ridicule my efforts and label me as being 'soft' on crime. I framed some of the cartoons and they are now on display above my top bookshelf in my study. In fact, I am rather proud of the controversies they created.

On another occasion, I led an "Anti-Death Penalty" march from the University of Nebraska campus to the steps of the state capitol where I gave my great (in my mind) "Make No Mistake" speech. It was a compilation of everything I had learned from Betsy and Jen at the evening dinner table and the university crowd loved it. On the other hand, the Governor let me know that since I wasn't "tough on crime" I would not be reappointed to serve another six year term on the Parole Board.

With these experiences in my background, you can understand my enthusiasm and delight in watching so many young people demonstrating and marching for causes they believe in today. But you'll never understand the great pride and sense of excitement that I felt as I watched Betsy sit at table on National-TV with Chuck Todd last month discuss 'Gun Control' on Meet The Press. Old memories flitted across my mind. It was an adult Betsy sitting at table like she did every night years ago when she was young, but now with a national audience. I thought to myself, "well, Chuck, you've met your match." Her years of sharpening iron against iron had not only prepared her for voicing her opinions but her engaging personality brought us all into concurrence with what she was saying. I was watching the "Meet The Press" show from home and found myself applauding and shouting out "BRAVO" at its ending.

A Beggar In Rajipur
Matthew 25:40

A poem I wrote while I was hiking up the Himalayas in India.

This beggar lying in the marketplace of old Ragipur
One among thousands of India's homeless poor,
Cried out to me with pleas of dire distress
Begging for alms to ease his helplessness;
Looking at me with hope that only Love understands
As if to say that his life was in my hands !

Then slowly the beggar inched away
Without the coins he hoped I'd cast his way;
And in my heart I heard the words I'd heard so often:
"Inasmuch as you do it unto the least of these, my Brethren"
And I knew then that Judgment lies in what love demands,
And that it was my life that was in the beggars hands !

Donald D. McCall

$\mathcal{A}$ "Fist Bump" Blessing
Genesis 32:26

One of my fondest memories of growing up in the mostly Moslem country of Lebanon was the habit of starting every day with prayer. It wasn't really a habit as much as the culturally enforced response to the sound of the Muezzin at the top of our neighborhood minaret crying out *"Allah Akbar"* at the top of his voice announcing the first **call to prayer** of a new day. It's a prayer discipline that I still maintain to this day. Barb chides me because I don't jump out of bed and immediately stand on my prayer rug as good Moslems do.... but I remind her that lying a bit longer in bed gives me more time to think loving thoughts about those for whom I am going to pray!

After Princeton and my ordination as a Presbyterian minster I accepted the invitation of a small church in the Midwest to become their Pastor. On my first Sunday I followed the Presbyterian liturgy found in The Book of Common Worship. After approaching the Chancel I climbed the steps up to the lectern (like a muezzin climbing the steps up to a minaret) and then I read the following printed **call to Worship:** *"Our help is in the name of the Lord who made heaven and earth."* A call which to me sounded very much like the muezzin's *"Allah Akbar"*. I wasn't disturbed by the similarity as much as I was by the feeling of separation and isolation that walking up to the Lectern had given me. I felt like I was a Protestant muezzin who had been chosen and set apart by God for this holy task. *Truth*

Donald D. McCall

is that I really wanted to be drawn closer to my congregation than to be
set aside by God.

After Princeton I went on to Luther Seminary to earn a further degree in Systematic Theology. At Luther, chapel services began with the clergy's Call to Worship with the minister saying: "The grace and peace of our Lord be with you all" after which the congregation responded by saying: "And also with you." Hearing the congregation respond was an instant revelation to me. It bonded clergy and congregation together as each group blessed the other. It was that sense of parity and unity that I had been seeking in worship and in my relationship with my congregation. It stems from the book of Genesis. After wrestling all night with an angel of the Lord ....and prevailing... Jacob said to the angel as morning was breaking: "I will not let you go until you bless me." (Gen 32:26) That is the same feeling I have after spending an hour on Sunday morning in church and listening to the sermon and then wrestling with the Word of God. And that's why I always reach out my hand to my pastor as he/she exits down the aisle or passes by during the recessional and I give them a "FIST BUMP" as if to say "I will not let you go until you bless me." Luther taught me that. One of the most important doctrines of the Reformation was Luther's "The Doctrine of the Priesthood of all Believers" namely that we are all spiritual priests to each other ...clergy or lay people... we are called to bless each other. I was reminded of the truth of that Doctrine recently while watching the funeral of President Bush and seeing the many people who reached out beyond the pews during the recessional to speak a word of blessing to the bereaved family.. It is that reaching out to bless one another that I find so appealing at Covenant Church. And I admire and listen in reverence and awe as our pastors so graciously incorporate Luther's dictum into our Presbyterian liturgy each week. Blessing each other is in many ways the highlight of a worship service for me. For example:

When I enter the sanctuary, John always has a bulletin and a hearing device ready for me and a smile that lets me know that he's glad to see me. I take that as a blessing. When I sit down in my pew Ruth always turns around from her pew seat in front of me and pats me on the forearm as if to say 'thank God we've made it through another week'. I consider that a blessing. Russell is the other bookend in our pew and we both are members of AKD an honorary Sociological society. His wife died recently and my grandchildren have adopted him as their honorary grandfather. We both consider that a blessing. Attorney Jim Ruhly sits on the other side of the sanctuary and after he is seated, he turns toward where I sit, smiles, nods his head and I nod back to hm.

That's how we exchange blessings. Brenda who often sits behind me always teases me by pulling at a tuft of my hair to let me know that she is thinking of me and I take that as a blessing. Joy, whose husband died 2 years ago, sits across the aisle from me always gives me a brief embrace before she leaves to let me know how much she misses her husband and we are both blessed by his memory. After the worship service granddaughter Claire brings my wheelchair down to our pew and then guides me out through the narthex to the front door to await Barb's bringing the car up to the porte-cochere. That's always a loving blessing! While I was waiting for Barb to arrive, I sensed someone standing behind me and soon I felt a hand on my left shoulder. I knew instinctively who it was. Jim Spilburg. I put my hand over his hand and I knew that God was blessing us both.

I write this to thank all of you for being such a blessing to me in this brief life that we share.....

Donald D. McCall

$\mathcal{B}$eing A Spendthrift
II Corinthians 12:15

I put some letters in the mail today and noticed with some embarrassment that although it was the first day of Spring, I was still using stamps that were designed for use during Christmas of last year. As you might guess I still have an abundance of those beautiful Madonna and Child stamps that depict the birth of our Lord in Bethlehem. I also have a reason and an explanation for that fact.. Last November I asked Barb to buy some stamps for our annual Christmas letter while she was out doing errands. I would like to believe that she bought a superabundance of stamps because she believes that we have that many friends to whom we send out Christmas greetings every year. But the truth is that Barb is an incorrigible **SPENDTHRIFT**. Now don't misunderstand me. That is not a denigrating word. In fact it is a very positive attribute. By definition, a Spendthrift is "someone who spends extravagantly".

In the Bible, extravagance in spending is often seen as a quality of selfless Love. In the story of the anointing of Jesus in Bethany, we read that a woman took a jar of very costly ointment and poured it's contents on Jesus' head **(Mark 14)** anointing Him in everyone's presence. Some of those sitting around the table became very angry at what they thought was a waste. They felt that they could have sold the ointment for a lot of money and then they could have given that money to the poor. But Jesus rebuked them and commended the woman for her extravagance. Then he said, "Wherever this story is told throughout the world, what she has done will be told in remembrance of her." Jesus said this act of a **SPENDTHRIFT** will always be remembered as a beautiful act of Love. And indeed it was.

I realized that the reason that I had an overabundance of Christmas stamps was because I was married to a **SPENDTHRIFT.** That is also why our living room is overstocked with toys and games for all the grandchildren. And why our cupboards are bursting with as many varieties of cereal that any child could ever hope to eat for breakfast. We have closets filled with skeins of wool for sweaters and mittens yet to be knit for children yet to be born. Barb's spendthrift philosophy is that you can't love too much. Every day is a new opportunity to lavish your love extravagantly upon others. And that doesn't mean just buying things. It also means "spending yourself" which is infinitely more intensive and difficult than the spending of money. Being a Spendthrift by spending yourself was a new insight that I came to understand only recently in two very dramatic moments.

1. After recently being hospitalized for a stroke I was working through the problems of paying some of my bills with the aid of Medicare. At the same time, for some unknown reason I came across the word of St. Paul who wrote to the Corinthians that children ought not to be expected to save up money for the care of their parents. **(II Corinthians 12:14)** Then I cam to the next verse that I realized was the heart and soul of Barb's Spendthrift philosophy: **"I will gladly spend and be spent for you." (II Corinthians 12:15)** I suddenly realized anew that St. Paul was characterizing a **SENDTHRIFT'S** life perfectly. I wondered how I could have lived with Barb for so long and not ascribed that text to her. Now I think I'll engrave it upon the lintel above the front door of our home so that all our guests will know what to expect when they come to visit us

Donald D. McCall

2. The second time that S. Paul's text came to my mind occurred at the time that I was hospitalized for the stroke that had taken me by surprise. That first night in the hospital I was dreading being all alone throughout the night. I said to Barb, "What if I have another stroke? Or even worse, what if I die?" She sensed the terror in my mind. Then she sat down on the edge of my hospital bed and cupped her hands and placed them on my cheeks with love that penetrated into my very soul she said, "I'm here to spend my life with you." And I thought now at last I know what love is. It is to spend and be spent for another. "**I will gladly spend and be spent for you**" Ah, I thought, those are the words that should be read during a wedding ceremony rather than the usual verses from I Corinthians 13. Then Barb pulled up an oversized chair and brought it to my bedside and there she curled up under blanket and spent the night at my side. That's the extravagance of Love. I cannot tell you what comfort it gave me to have her there next to me all night long....and it was a long night!

I learned more about the extravagance of Love in those past two experiences than I ever learned in any graduate seminar or classroom. And I can understand the prediction of Jesus that a woman's simple act of extravagant love would be remembered throughout all history. And I also learned that having a Stroke was for me a 'Stroke of Luck' because it gave me a new insight into the meaning of being anointed with Love.

*P*ilate's Predicament
John 18:38

I had the good fortune to be invited to a World Council of Churches meeting in Geneva, Switzerland some years ago. I thought that it might be a good opportunity to have my Senior High School son Russell join me and gain a firsthand experience of such an international event. My hidden agenda was to also take some vacation time in order to show Russell some of the historic sights of Europe. On our first free afternoon, we took the train ride down to the other end of Lake Geneva to tour the ancient Castle of Chillon. It's deep dungeon housed religious prisoners during the time of the Reformation, including Francois Bonivard who was a friend to John Calvin. Francois was burned at the stake but three of his sons were imprisned at Chillon from 1532 to 1536. It was of their imprisonment that the English poet Lord Byron in 1816 wrote the long 392 line classic poem **"The Prisoner of Chillon"**. It tells of their years of suffering and of two of the three sons dying while chained to their pillars. What I remember of the poem, which I first read during my childhood years, are the last few lines spoken by the only surviviing son of Francois Bonivard. They have made a lasting impression on my life.

> *"At last men came to set me free*
> *I ask'd not why, and reck'd not where*

Donald D. McCall

It was at length the same to me
Fetter'd or fetterless to be
My very chains and I grew friends
So much a long commmunion tends to make us what
we are."

I have used that quote over and over again in both the Pulpit and when chairing Nebraska State Board of Parole hearings. It is at the heart of the Gospel. It answerd the quintessential question that **Pilate** put to Jesus; "**What is truth?**" (John 18:38) Or what is the key to a meaningful and productive life? Which is also the primary question in our geo-political world today. Or philosophically speaking, 'What constitutes the basis of authenticity in life?" Jesus answered Pilate's question simply through his presence. "I am the way and the **TRUTH** and the life." Pilate was looking face to face with the answer to his question, but he couldn't see it. His wife knew that he was being pressured by political fores and so she warned him: *Have nothing todo with this man, for I have suffered many things this day in a dream because of this innocent man."* *(Matt 27:19)* "But Pilate paid no heed to her advice (*Now there is a sermon somewhere in that text…but I have yet to preach it!*) and instead he washed his hands as if to recuse himself from the case and consequently Christ was condemned to die on the Cross. But the answer to Pilates question lives on.

As Christ explained it to his disciples let me here paraphrase it for you. If you seek a meaningful life….if you are seeking the TRUTH… then come and abide with me….live with me….for it's that long encounter that intimate **communion of friends ….** **that tends to make us what we are.** (John 15:4-11). An authentic life is a life that is borne out abding in Christ. Not in wisdom, knowledge, nor in assent to a concept but rather it is what I would call a personal relationship….abiding… as Jesus said: "Abide in me as I abide in you". **Yes, it's that long communion of being a part** of each other's life, abiding in one another, that tends to make us what we are."

If you travel east fom Lake Geneva past Interlaken you will come to Lake Lucerne and a range of mountains including **Mt. Pilatus.** Tradition holds that Pontius Pilate was buried in a small lake at the foot of Mt. Pilatus. History (Josephus) records that Pilate was a man of 'furious and vindictive temperment' who was a blend of self will wherein he relished insulting the local authorities. Philo records that Pilate's term as Prefect of Judea ended when a large group of Samaritans had gone up to Mt Gerizem to look at some historical artifacts datng back to the time of Moses. As they began their ascent they encountered a batallion of Pilate's heavily armed infantryman who had been sent to deter them and in the ensuing battle Jews were killed and others took flight. The Samaritans filed a complaint with Vitellius, the Roman Governor of Syria who then ordered Pilate to be taken to Rome to explain his actions to Tiberius. Unfortunately, by the time Pilate arrived in Rome, Tiberius had died. Pilate then suffered one misfortune after another under the reign of Caligula (AD 37-41) Legend states that he committed suicide and that his body was thrown into the Tiber river but the waters were so disturbed that they took the body and threw it into a small lake at the foot of **Mt. Pilatus** where the body is said to emerge every year on Good Friday to wash its hands.

I remember these stories from the days of my youth, the sites I have visited, the books I have read and the events I have experienced. **I am writing to you now individually to <u>thank you</u> for being someone who has shared my life…who has decorated my life… and whose long communion has made me who I am.** And I want to thank you as I now enter my Ninetieth year for having made my life so fulfilled and so meaningful for me !

Donald D. McCall

$\mathcal{A}$cknowledging Others
Ephesians 1:3-6

I had the privilege of preaching on Good Friday and as I stepped up to the pulpit I realized anew how much I enjoyed preaching and also how long it had beens since I last had the opportunity to do what I was born to do. In fact I had to buy a new shirt for the occasion inasmuch as this was not a 'High Church' pulpit and I didn't wear my gown and Geneva tabs. The pleasure of preaching lingered with me throughout the week and reminded me of a lifetime of fulfillment I found in preaching and later in teaching Homiletics (The Art of Preaching) to aspiring young preachers to be.

Later that week Barb presented me with a new book she had earlier ordered through Amazon as a surprise for me. It was a book by Anna Carter Florence whom I knew when I was in Rochester and she was in Minneapolis and who is now the professor of Homiletics at Columbia Seminary in Georgia. What intrigued me more than the books contents were the three pages of 'acknowledgements' that she listed in the preface. I counted almost 80 names of people whom she thanked for guiding her and mentoring her in the course of her life. I suddenly realized how negligent I had been in writing my books for not having 'acknowledged' or thanked enough of the people who had guided me and helped me write and preach in my early career. They were my Mentors and I should have acknowledged them. Maybe it because at the time I didn't realize they were mentoring me.

I know that I have always publicly acknowledged my thanks to some of my Univ. of Glasgow who always treated me like his long lost relative from America. Dr. Stewart at the Univ. of Edinburgh who patiently taught me the true essence of preaching. Dr. Fritch of Princeton whose books have a special place on my shelf and who was also my doubles tennis partner. And of course, My Father who enabled and encouraged me all the days of my life. However, that leaves about 80 other people still unmentioned. Unlike Anna Carter Florence I will not attempt to name them but I do want to for the first time in my life publicly express my thanks to the Session of the First Presbyterian Church in Tecumseh.

It was my first parish. There were six elders on the Session. One was a gravedigger. One was among the wealthiest members of town. One was a crop duster. One was a farmer. One was a businessman and one was retired. I had come directly from Pinceton and had many brilliant ideas as to what the church ought to be. They nixed them all! I saw them not as <u>mentors</u> but rather as <u>tormentors</u>!

After about two years in the community and after having involved myself strongly in various civic capacities the State Senator from our district retired and his seat in the Unicameral was open for any new candidate. I jumped at the opportunity and felt that I was eminently qualified, but I needed Session approval for the time it would take away from the parish. I thought that they would be thrilled that I was willing to take on such an added responsibility. The Session discussed it briefly and then asked to vote by written ballot. I didn't see why they needed to have a secret ballot for such an obvious decision. Nonetheless, we cut up some paper ballots and they all wrote their response to my request. The clerk read the votes... one by one...It was a unanimous NO. I was not only shocked but also visibly dismayed. Then they began to explain their decision and in so many words they said, "You were born to preach. "and we are not going to do anything that would allow you to be distracted from your destiny." I went home that evening feeling totally defeated. My

Donald D. McCall

Board of Tormentors had totally destroyed my hopes and dreams. It was beyond me to understand.

It took me a long time to realize that often when we feel that the very foundations of our hopes and dreams are being shaken, we discover later that it is God who is shaking them. Therefore,, let me acknowledge belatedly my thanks to that Session, those truly great God fearing mentors in that small rural church in Nebraska.

Resonating
Luke 7:36-50

Last month Barb made several trips to Omaha as the pro-bono executor of her Aunt Rosie's estate which included the sale of two homes and disposing of their contents. In one home she found a grand piano on the second floor and then a cello in the attic. Knowing that I had played the violin my whole life, (while secretly wishing in my heart that I owned a cello,) Barb then carefully packed the cello in the back of our van and brought it home to me here in Madison. After having it restrung and restored she presented it to me, much to my delight, saying "Now the 'Big Guy' can finally own a 'Big Violin'." I loved it instantly. We were perfectly matched ....dare I say...even destined for each other. Here I am in the early morning: in my bedroom, in my bathrobe and <u>into</u> my cello.

Donald D. McCall

Oddly enough, the **New Yorker** magazine, on the same weekend that Barb gifted me with my new cello, ran an article about Matt Haimovitz, the world renown cellist who had accidentally dropped his 17th century multimillion dollar cello and it's neck broke. He doubted that it could be restored yet he took it to a cello repair shop near Columbus Circle to see what could be done. The New Yorker article described Haimovitz's anxiety as he went to the repair shop months later to retrieve the old cello he had been playing for thirty years. He wondered if the restored instrument would still resound with the same ravishingly beautiful tones that the world had come to love during his concerts. His cello had been in the hands of luthiers and he knew that the relationship between a cello and a cellist was unusually and singularly tight. *"You have to wrap yourself around the cello while playing"* he said, *"You have to be good friends... **intimate** friends."*. A cello is an instrument whose sounds are closest to the human voice in range and more than any other instrument it **resonates** <u>with</u> the artist playing it rather than **responding** <u>to </u>the score alone. You can feel it resonating in your knees and throughout your whole body as each note is played. Resonance is an aspect of that multi-dimensionality that every cellist must learn to use and Matt Haimovitz wondered as he approached the repair studio if he and his old cello still maintained that same powerful and heartfelt paradigmatic relationship that had enthralled audiences throughout the world. When he sat down with his repaired cello, he wrapped himself around it slowly and began playing a few scales. Then he launched into a Bach Suite while leaning in to listen. Gradually it began resonating with the same sounds and vibrations that Haimovitz had been hoping to sense and hear. He looked up, smiled and accepted a congratulatory glass of wine. Cellos **resonate**…that's beyond responding…as much as a Kiss is beyond a handshake!

It then came to my mind that when **Jesus** calls us to follow Him, our first thought is to **respond** positively to His call. But now, through my intimacy with my new cello, I've come to understand that what Jesus really wants is an *intimate* encounter with me…a union that **resonates** with my whole being, that is in sync with all that I am. St. Luke (7:36-50) explains it to us this way: One of the Pharisees invited Jesus into his house to have dinner with him. Jesus entered the home and the sat down at the table to eat. Just then a woman who was a sinner knelt down at the feet of Jesus and began to wash his feet with her tears, kissing them and anointing them with precious ointment. When the Pharisee saw what was happening and what kind of woman that it was who was with Jesus he was aghast. But before he could have his servants put her away, Jesus said: **"Simon, I have something to say to you. When I entered your home you gave me no water for my feet. But she**

Donald D. McCall

has bathed my feet with her tears and dried them with her hair. You gave me no kiss, but she has not stopped kissing my feet. You did not anoint my head with oil but she has anointed me with precious ointment. I tell you that her sins (which are many) are forgiven because she has shown great love." It was a love that resonated through the whole room but Simon couldn't feel it. I can understand that. I played a violin for years but I never felt music resonate throughout my whole body as it does when I play the cello and my knees tremble!

I've come to think of this a lot lately, now that I have a cello. Especially on those occasions at church **when Jesus invites us to sit at table with him**. The Communion Service is the Holiest of all invitations. The question is whether we **respond** to the invitation or whether we **resonate** with great Love for the opportunity to share life together. Sometimes I feel as if in responding to the directions in our approaching the table we miss the opportunity to focus on function over form. Are we listening to the text: *"All that are truly sorry for their sins and desire to delivered of them are invited and encouraged to come to this sacrament."* Or are we listening to the minister tell us how to respond when he says: "We ask you to come forward down the center aisle (not easy with a cane) approach an Elder at the chancel steps. Take a piece of bread from the paten (plain or gluten free). Then take a cup after which please dispose of it in the wastebasket on the side aisle and ascend back up to your pew. There is a difference in **responding** to instructions and in **resonating** with a desire to have your life be in tune with the life of Christ. My cello taught me that! And the woman who was a sinner taught me that there is a world of difference between a welcoming handshake and a kiss !

The Death Of A Beloved Friend
II Kings 13:20-25

I lost a dear friend last month and I am still grieving. At my age, I don't have many (if any) 'Dear around to share such a trusted relationship in life. Bill King was one of them. I first met Bill back in the 60's when he was Friends.' left. Intimacy in a friendship demands a history of continuity as well as comradery. In my 90h year on this planet I can count on my right hand the number of 'Dear Friends' that are still a newly ordained pastor accepting his first call to ministry at Winona MN. I was the elderly ensconced head of staff at Rochester MN. I liked him instantly. An ardent Calvinist with a Jesuit's mind, a Missionary zeal, setting a high bar for his calling and always with an Irish limerick lurking somewhere in the shadow of his smile. In his second year at Winona, he invited me to preach at his church during a mid-week Lenten series and I enjoyed it immensely. You can tell a lot about a minister just by entering his pulpit. I could sense that evening that he was "Beloved" by his congregation. I also realized that evening that it was at that point that we differed in our roles as ministers. I never felt that I was "Beloved" by my congregation. I always felt highly respected but never considered myself "Beloved." Maybe my aloofness was because I wore a clerical collar with preaching tabs; Doctoral stripes on my gown; and had to mount isolating steps to get into my pulpit … or maybe it just wasn't in my DNA.

Donald D. McCall

Time moves on. Bill went his own way and I went mine. We met occasionally at Synod or national meetings and always with an eagerness to 'catch up' inasmuch as our early years together had formed the track and tenure of our careers with a collegial bonding strong enough to last a lifetime. Then a decade ago when Barb and I sold our Lincoln home and moved to Madison to be closer to the grandchildren, we were invited by Betsy to attend Covenant church. The first Sunday we went there we walked through the front door and ran directly into Bill and Mary in the narthex! Somewhat shocked and wondrously excited we all embraced and I also remembered that Bill was the "Beloved" Pastor Emeritus of Covenant Church. We quickly picked up anew toward the end of our lives, that affirming relationship established in our formative years. Thereafter we never had tine enough, or words enough to finish a conversation. One evening we had invited Bill and Mary to our 3rd floor apartment home for dinner. After they arrived Bill had his Irish drink and I had my Scotch on ice as we sat on the deck and watched the sun slowly set. When Barb went into the kitchen to get more 'ice' for our drinks she sensed that things weren't quite right in the oven and in opening the oven door she realized that the roast chicken was still cold....so we enjoyed the condiments and the desert but most of all the uninterrupted conversation of the evening. Not a Biblical Miracle, but a memorable meatless meal, which had turned into a feast of friendship.

Scripture records that in earlier times Prophets and Priests were anointed, as are ministers ordained today as they receive the mantle of their calling. That anointing in the Old Testament was a sign of God loving them with a love that lasted even beyond death. I thought of that when I attended Bill's funeral a few days ago. My mind traveled back to the time that the prophet "Elisha died and they buried him. Now bands of Moabites used to invade the land in the spring of the year. As the man was being buried a marauding band was seen approaching and so they threw the dead man into the grave of Elisha. As soon as the man's body touched the bones of

Elisha, the man came to life and stood on his feet." (II Kings 13:20-21) That ancient story from the Old Testament came into my mind while I was sitting in our family pew awaiting the beginning of Bill's Memorial Service. Not to be sacrilegious... I thought if anyone can make an evening dinner without 'the meat' become a memorable festival he can also make a dead man stand on his feet. As you think of it, that is exactly what Bill did for the Covenant congregation. He brought them to life...he gave them new life....he gave them his life!

The last time I saw Bill was the Sunday before his hospitalization. He was quite bent over while he was talking to one of the older members of our congregation. His body was bent, not because of osteoporosis or scoliosis, but like me his hearing was weakening with age and he was getting his ear as close to his friends face as he could. I looked at him and smiled to myself and thought "Bill, you can't get any closer to your parishioners than you've always been for all these years. That's why they Love you. That's why you're a 'Pastor Emeritus'. It means Beloved." And so you are...so you are....

Farewell, my Beloved Friend.

Donald D. McCall

Why I Write
Mark 6:34

Lately my ten-year old computer became so obtusely obstinate that I couldn't even get the mouse to go chase its own cheese. Obviously, it was obsolete! A couple of years ago I thought about buying a new one, but I was afraid that my demise would precede its warranty expiration date. Typically, a Scotsman's decision.

Then, a few days later, Barb walked into my study carrying a huge new 27" Apple iMac Computer with more bells and whistles than **I** ever dreamed possible. It has a widescreen LED backlit Retina 5K with 2880-pixel ambient light sensors. It took us the rest of the day to get it all assembled.

Surprisingly, by then my mouse had gone on to his eternal reward and replacing him was a small "*magic trackpad*" that responds to all my commands with the touch of my forefinger.

My feeble protests that she shouldn't have spent so much money on somebody my age and all of my verbal protestations were quickly and visibly overridden by the expressions of joy and exuberance that I couldn't hold back. Barb gave me a quick kiss on the forehead and then said, "*I know how frustrated you were with your old computer, so I bought you this one because I want you to keep on writing.*"

It took a moment for those words to register in my mind. She wanted me to keep on writing. I suddenly realized that is **<u>why</u> she did what she did was more important to me than <u>what</u> she did**.

She was motivated by her love for me and her desire to respond lovingly to my needs while simultaneously encouraging me at my age to keep on writing!

That interchange with Barb changed my whole exegetical understanding of Scripture. I had never thought of **motivation** as being at the heart and core of the Gospels. I've spent a lifetime preaching about the miracles that Jesus performed… the words that Jesus spoke….the doctrines that he entrusted us….the sacrifice of His life upon the cross….the sacraments we still share in our church life….all that **He did** for us without fully understanding **why He did** what He did for us. What **motivated** Him? Oh, I knew that it was Love. But I had never personalized that Love. Now my mind keeps flashing back to my surprising response in receiving the new computer that Barb bought for me and realizing what had motivated her, <u>**why**</u> **she did what she did became more important to me than** <u>**what**</u> **she did**.

That realization brought me to a new interpretive understanding of Scripture. I no longer read scripture to seek textual or historical understanding of what Jesus said or did but now I read scripture seeking to understand why He said or did what He did. I have discovered that in every case it was to respond lovingly to the needs of others. That's what love does. It motivates you **to respond lovingly to another's needs.**

For example: When Jesus and his disciples were seeking a quiet place to be alone, a crowd followed them and after some time he **looked out lovingly at the crowd** and realized that they were probably hungry and so He resolved their problem and fed them. It's not the miracle of the feeding of the 5000. It's the miracle of the power of Love. Why Jesus did what He did was because **He loved them**. (Mark 6:34}

At another time a rich man came to Jesus and asked Him what he had to do to inherit eternal life. "Jesus looked at him **lovingly**" and then told him to sell what he owned and give his money to the poor. He answered the man's question about eternal life because **He Loved him**. (Mark 10:26)

On another occasion as He was leaving the city of Jericho a great crowd followed him. Two blind men cried out to him begging to be healed. Moved with compassion (**Love) for them** He touched their eyes and they regained their sight and they followed Him. (Matthew 20:34) He healed them because He loved them.

In the village of Nain he encountered a funeral procession. It was a widow's only son. She was weeping in deep distress. Jesus looked at her he had great **compassion (love) for her** and then said, "Do not weep" and then he touched the bier and the young man was raised to life. (Luke 7:13)

In every case each account of a miracle is preceded by **Jesus** looking with Love or Compassion upon those in need. Therefore I am now more impressed…more moved … by what motivated Jesus to do what He did than by the fact of what He did. I'd follow that Love anywhere! As with Barb's gift to me of a new computer, w<u>hy</u> **she did what she did became more important to me than <u>what</u> she did.**

By now I'm sure you've guessed why I'm writing you this letter. It's to remind you, "Ma Habibis" that <u>**why**</u> **I write you is more important than <u>what</u> I write."** I write you because it gives me great pleasure when putting pen to paper **to look out lovingly upon you** in my mind and remember with thanksgiving, your impact upon on my life.

*L*et Conscience Be Your Guide
John 8:9-10 KJV

The **Book of Psalms** begins with these words: "*Happy are they who delight in the law of the Lord, and on His law they meditate day and night.*" Frankly, I've discovered that such meditation is almost always at night. That's when in the moments of my insomnia the Law seeks me out to convict me of some very minor as well as some very egregious violations of God's laws in my life. And since it's my own conscience that convicts me there is no way I can escape the judgment of such condemnation. Such is the power of the conscience which consummates the dark hours of the soul until night turns into morning light.

Theologically speaking the conscience is hard to define. It's an intuitive Divine faculty that assists us in distinguishing right from wrong. Unlike the appendix it is not something that can surgically be removed from the body. It is inherent in all of us and in all that we do. I was first introduced to the concept of a conscience through the 1940 move "*Pinocchio*". Jiminy Cricket (a minced misnomer for Jesus Christ) was a wise companion who sat on

Pinocchio's shoulder like a 'good conscience' and whispered good advice in Pinocchio's ear throughout all of his adventures telling him to "**let his conscience be his guide.**"

In Sunday School we read about the working of the human conscience in the story of the Pharisees who had caught a woman in

Donald D. McCall

the act of adultery and according to the law of Moses they were ready to stone her to death at which time Jesus suggested that he who is without sin should be the one to cast the first stone. *"And they which heard it,* **being convicted by their own conscience**, *went out one by one, beginning at the eldest, even unto the last: and Jesus was left alone, and the woman standing in the midst."* (**John 8:9-10 KJV**) That's how the conscience wrestled with it until I was exhausted.

When I was at Princeton studying **Calvin's** Institutes I came to understand that Calvin saw **conscience** as a 'Battleground' where our human will is constantly fighting the will if God. I found myself spending most of my time and energy waging war against myself in a non-productive battle with God. Then later studying in Scotland I was further ensconced in that same war with the Devil enhanced by John **Knox's** temerity to challenge the Queen with the need to further "educate her conscience." The rule of conscience was rapidly becoming the focus of my spiritual life. A few years later I attended **Luther** Seminary in Minnesota to earn a further degree in Systematic Theology. It was for me a spiritual awakening. One day in class I heard a professor quoting Luther say: "**The anguish of conscience is the beginning of Faith.**" That sentence had the ring of truth to it. I wrote it down. I spent a year studying what it meant. I came to the conclusion that the conscience was not a destructive Calvinistic battleground where I wrestled with the will of God but rather it was like Luther suggested, a profound instructive opportunity to listen to the voice of God. Insomnia became for me, not a 'Battleground' but a moment in the night when Jesus would waken me and say, "Donald, we need to talk." It always reminded me of my days at Princeton when I was an after class taxi-cab driver and I would see Dr. Kuist taking one of his evening walks and I would drive up toward him and ask if I could walk with him. Then we would walk and talk and I learned more from him than I ever learned in his classroom. It was an interruption of my needed taxicab income but those walks and talks remain with me to this day as one of the most productive and memorable of my Princeton days. Likewise insomnia, when Jesus wakes me now and interrupts my needed sleep, I eagerly go and walk with Him and talk to Him and He helps me discern and understand the path I need to take. I must tell you that one time as we were walking and talking I looked over and noticed that Jesus was smiling. I returned the smile. His smile grew wider and I couldn't hold back a muffled laugh. His return laughter was overwhelming and we just stood there in the middle of the road embracing in laughter. I woke Barb to tell her about what had just happened. It was a sense of bonding and loving acceptance that I had never experienced before in my life. It was too real to dismiss. It was GRACE overriding the LAW. The heart of the Gospel. I still smile as I think of it. Analogously, it was as if Jiminy Cricket had jumped off my shoulder and into my heart.

I must stop at this point and admit that I realize that the concept of a working conscience is not a popular or readily accepted idea among a younger generation which believes in doing the expedient thing (situation ethics) rather than the right thing. It's as if they haven't studied or read about the conscience in their Bibles. And they probably haven't. The version of the Bible I used above is the **King James** edition printed in **1612.** It's been used for centuries. The **RSV** Version of the Bible (in our pew racks) was printed in **1952** and it deleted the phrase "**being convicted of their own conscience**" No wonder there is no understanding of a working conscience if the only mention of it in the Gospels has been deleted. (Check and compare your Bible with the King James Edition) Which is why I write to you: To let an old man remind you of an old and basic truth, even though it's deleted from your modern Bible: "**Let your conscience be your guide.**"

Donald D. McCall

$\mathscr{A}$t The Foot Of The Cross
Matthew 27:46

Speaking theologically, the Doctrine of the **Incarnation** (Christmas) and the Doctrine of the **Atonement** (Easter) indissolubly bound together as one. So says John Calvin, Karl Barth, Emil Brunner and all of my professors in Seminary. Jesus knew it too and called it out from the cross: "***For this I was born.***" Matt. 27:46 (in the Aramaic Translation) It took years to hammer that fact into our heads and then it was the first truth that we ignored when we clambered up the steps to our own pulpits. I've never preached a sermon about death on a Christmas morning nor have we ever displayed a crèche at Easter. Thus the opening sentence of this letter is the dilemma that I find myself in as I start to write to you about Christ's death on the Cross this year at Christmastide.

My thinking on this subject all began a few years ago when I was chairing the **Board of Parole** in Nebraska. We were preparing for an execution at the Penitentiary and someone asked me where I wanted to sit as an official observer in the execution chamber. I responded that I had no intention of observing someone else's death in the electric chair. Especially not the death of a man whom I had come to know as a friend. Furthermore, I had already witnessed one execution and it was forever ensconced in my mind. It was in a former life…years ago when I was a teenager at a church camp on the Platte River in Nebraska. Young minds are easily swayed. I had never been to a 'Sunday School' nor to a 'Church Camp' while growing up in my mostly Moslem homeland of Lebanon. Church Camp" was a totally new experience for me.

One evening at church camp as we gathered for evening devotionals we all sat around the campfire and sang an old African American Plantation Hymn, "**<u>Were You There When They Crucified My Lord</u>**" I was strangely overcome by that experience and **in my dreams that night I was transported to Golgatha** on the outskirts of Jerusalem. The scene was very real to me. I was more than happy to be back in my homeland. I remember breathing through my mouth to capture the oral sweet smell of the cyclamen, the cedars and the pines. Then I noticed **three crosses** rising on a hill ahead of me. People had gathered around them. The man in the middle was the center of attention and I immediately recognized Him from all our church camp literature. What I saw was the Jesus whom we had been singing about that night at the campfire. The scene was so frightful that it had caused me to tremble. As I watched, I soon came to notice that others had gathered there at the foot of the cross:.

Many were just people **passing by**. Observers who had no idea as to what they were experiencing. They were in the midst of a moment of kairos in human history and casually walked through it without seeing it. There were **soldiers** at the foot of the cross casting lots to divide the few earthly possessions Jesus had owned. They were so blinded by their desire for earthly things that they had no idea of the gift of Gods' love that was hovering above them. There were **Chief Priests, Scribes and Elders** who wagged their heads and threw his own words back at Him saying, "He saved others. Himself he cannot save! He trusted in God…Let God save Him!" There was a **Centurian,** a Captain in the Roman army who supervised the crucifixion and was experienced in such matters. He was a just man and his observation was, "Surely this man is innocent". There was a **Thief** on a nearby cross who in repenting of his sins cried out to Jesus "Lord, remember me when you come into your kingdom". And

Donald D. McCall

Jesus responded, "This day thou shalt be with me in paradise". There were a **Few Women** huddled together apart from the crowd: Mary, the mother of Jesus. Mary Magdalene. Mary the wife of Cleophas. The only Disciple there was **John**… the 'Beloved Disciple'.

There were others **not recorded** in Scripture. **Neither is what I saw next recorded in Holy Writ.** After Jesus had breathed his last, from the corner of my eye, I saw John the Beloved Disciple go to Mary, the mother of Jesus who was sitting with the other women and he helped her to her feet. Then I saw John reach out his arm and place it around Mary's shoulder to comfort her on the long journey homeward. It was a loving thing to do. It was the love of heaven made known to us in this earthly life. It was the love of God made known on the cross that spilled out for us to see and understand it in human form. It was the Love of God **BORN** in Bethlehem of Judea (the **Incarnation)** and also **BORNE** upon the cross (**the Atonement**) at Golgatha in Jerusalem. It was the love we were to see in Jesus and adopt as our own as we reach out to one another and put our arms around each other on our homeward journeys in this life. It's the Love that you have shared with me over the years and which I now cherish more than ever before. It's the Love that Christina Rossetti wrote about in 1885 in her hymn, which I have used as the Worship Service Benediction every Christmas Sunday for well over 60 years:

"Love came down at Christmas;
Love all lovely, Love Divine;
Love was born at Christmas;
Love be yours and Love be mine"

$\mathcal{A}$ Benediction
John 21:15

I began this book with a dedication page acknowledging my love as well as my debt to my daughter Kate. I have come to realize that In our lives our children often teach us through their love for us more than we realize or than we are able to intellectually process. Having thus started this book with that prolegomenon, I now realize that I need to end it with an equally notable word of appreciation to Kate and you readers. Thus, I will close with this Benediction, an old Latin word meaning "Good (bene) Word (dictum)" often used as a parting blessing ... or in the case of writing this book, you might see it as a summary or 'Last Word'.

In my own mind I cannot help referring back to an old quote from T. S. Eliot, a British poet of World War II, who wrote *"The end of all our exploring* (philosophical searching*) will be to arrive where we started and to know the place for the first time."*

I feel that all that I have written is something that I have always known, but which I now see in a new or different context due to my 90 years of life.... life with my extended family and many of you who are reading this. However, since this is a book about Love returning Love, let me leave you with the same text with which I began and with this photo of Kate and me living out our response to the Apostle John's text in real life!

Donald D. McCall

THE END

Printed in the United States
By Bookmasters